SIGENA:

ROMANESQUE PAINTINGS
IN SPAIN AND THE ARTISTS
OF THE WINCHESTER BIBLE

BY WALTER OAKESHOTT

Frontispiece: Head of Her. Wall painting from the Chapter House at Sigena

Walter Oakeshott

Fraser

SIGENA

Romanesque Paintings in Spain

& the Winchester Bible Artists

WITH 227 ILLUSTRATIONS

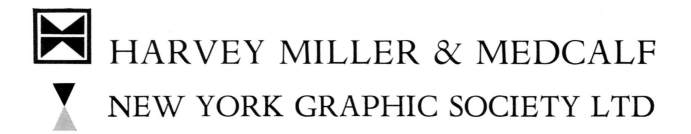

HARVEY MILLER & MEDCALF

NEW YORK GRAPHIC SOCIETY LTD

© 1972 Harvey Miller & Medcalf Ltd

56 Doughty Street · London WC1 · England

Published in the United States and Canada by

New York Graphic Society Ltd, Greenwich, Connecticut

STANDARD BOOK NUMBER 8212-0497-1

LIBRARY OF CONGRESS CATALOG CARD NUMBER 72-85588

Edited and designed by Elly Miller

Printed at The Curwen Press · Plaistow · London · England

Contents

Preface

The present publication on the wall paintings from the Chapter House at Sigena and their relationship to the Winchester Bible and its artists has afforded me the opportunity of carrying into a new phase the study of a subject which first interested me more than forty years ago. Developing over so long a period, one's ideas inevitably owe much to other people; and indeed, if I may put it that way, the main progress of the story is primarily their achievement, not mine. But my own great opportunity came in the thirties, when I was responsible for organising in Winchester an exhibition of 'Winchester' illumination; an exhibition which included not only the Winchester Bible itself, but also the leaf from the Morgan Library in New York, which Dr. Eric Millar had recognised recently as having been illuminated by Winchester artists. The scepticism of Mr. A. J. Collins, Dr. Millar's predecessor as Keeper of Manuscripts in the British Museum, made a great impression on me: we knew nothing, he said, for certain about any of these artists, where they worked, who they were, or who were their patrons.

Since that time, the individuality of the various hands represented in the decoration of the Bible, has been a continuing preoccupation. Having formed the view, on stylistic grounds, that some illuminations were designed in a different hand from that which painted them, I was baffled how to prove it. It was that wonderful scholar, Fritz Saxl, who devised a brilliantly successful method of showing up, and photographing, the drawings below the paint. Two American scholars, L. W. Jones and C. R. Morey, had suggested some time before that the artist responsible for two full pages of drawings still in the Bible, had also worked on a famous twelfth-century copy of Terence. Their work was a pre-requisite for a satisfactory analysis of the relationship of the Morgan Leaf to the Bible. A chance remark made long before, by Dr. M. R. James, put me onto the track, in a country house in Yorkshire, of one of the initials that had been cut out of the Bible and lost. It is now sewn back in its place. I produced my small book on the *Artists of the Winchester Bible* in 1945. If it had had no other result, the fact that it led to Dr. Otto Pächt's identifying, as the work of Winchester artists, the paintings at Sigena which are the subject of this book, would have made it worth writing. In it, I mentioned tentatively the possibility that one of them (this very Master of the Morgan Leaf) might have seen the mosaics at Cefalù in Sicily. Dr. Otto Demus's book on the Sicilian mosaics appeared soon after, with its precise documentation and dating of that material and this has made feasible the attempt to study the possibility in detail; with the moral support of his view, there expressed, that two of the Winchester Bible artists had looked at them. Professor

1 and 2. The Convent at Sigena, Huesca

Francis Wormald had pointed to the significance, for the study of Byzantine influences in England, of two full pages in a Byzantinising style included in a Psalter decorated in Winchester soon after the middle of the twelfth century. And Dr. Neil Ker, in his *English Manuscripts in the Century after the Conquest*, not only examined what are in my view some of the most hopeful criteria for dating the Bible; but also, by observing that the hand of one of its correctors occurred also in a splendid Bible in the Bodleian (and indeed that one must suppose the two actually to have lain side by side at some time when they were being corrected) put me on to the importance of a style of rubrication to be seen in both; and also at Sigena. To two Spanish scholars, Dr. Gudiol and Dr. Ainau, it is due that the Sigena paintings were photographed just in time, and that the remains of them after the fire were rescued and pieced together. All these scholars I have had the privilege of meeting. Some have been intimate friends. Without their generous help, the ideas worked out in this book would never have taken shape, and it is dedicated to Otto Pächt, who made the key discovery: a small tribute to his noteworthy contribution, in this field and so many others.

My special thanks are due also to the Dean and Chapter of Winchester. They made me their Honorary Librarian while I was Headmaster of Winchester College, and this afforded a chance of studying the Bible, over an extended period, such as no one else has had. I would like also to thank the present librarian, Canon Amand de Mendieta; the archivist, Canon Bussby; and the Assistant Librarian, Miss B. N. Forder, for their unfailing help. Mrs. Elizabeth Bury exquisitely copied for this book lettering from Winchester and from Sigena which is an important part of its argument, and has helped on many points of style. The Leverhulme Trust made possible a visit to New York in which I renewed an acquaintance with the Leaf that had begun so long before. And I am deeply indebted to the editor of this book, Mrs. Elly Miller, for the perceptiveness and understanding of what it is all about, that have played so large a part in its production.

OXFORD, 1972   WALTER OAKESHOTT

Introduction

In the year 1936, when the Spanish authorities were making a photographic record of the medieval wall paintings in Spanish churches, the task of photographing the paintings in the Chapter House of the Convent of Sigena was assigned to Señor J. Gudiol. Up to that date these paintings were comparatively little known; partly perhaps because of their unusual character. They fitted uncomfortably into the Romanesque category, and equally uncomfortably into the Gothic; and they were so unlike most Spanish medieval wall paintings that even the country of origin of the artists was questioned. Moreover the convent was not altogether easy of access. West of Barcelona, the ground rises steeply into broken rocky hills, through which the road winds westwards, and before the days of motor roads, the journey was neither rapid nor easy. Sigena is some hundred and fifty miles from Barcelona, beyond Lerida. In the region round it, the nature of the landscape changes to high, desolate uplands, which have been extensively eroded into a broad and fertile river valley that is said to contain some of the best farm land in this part of Spain. The valley is guarded, in its approach, by sheer buttresses of soft, eroded rock looking like the apse of a fortified cathedral thrusting out into it; with layers of coloured earth, red and purple, among the ochre. The convent itself, a royal foundation, was established in this rich but isolated region by the Queen of Aragon, Doña Sancha, in 1183.

Gudiol was astonished by the quality of what he saw in the Chapter House. Here was no series of fragments such as are often the only reward of the search for medieval wall paintings, but a great scheme of decoration, still preserving its splendid colour, deep blues, rose, and greens dominating the impression it produced; while the ceiling of wood was in a Spanish Moorish style, carved in patterns in relief (Ill. 9) and gilded and coloured in a way which set off magnificently the deeper tones of the paintings. Not only the arches, but the walls also were covered with paintings, though many of these latter were hidden by whitewash. The painting of the *Presentation in the Temple* he himself partly cleaned. The *Crucifixion* painting could, for the moment, only be explored by the preliminary cleaning of details here and there; but this made it clear that it was a masterpiece. Gudiol made a photographic record (though good colour emulsions were, alas, not yet available) of all that was so far visible, and left the rest for attention when more cleaning should have been done. But the civil war had started. Three months later, the Chapter House, and many of the other buildings of the Convent, were roofless rubble. In the Chapter House itself, there had been an appalling fire. What remained of the paintings (on three of the four

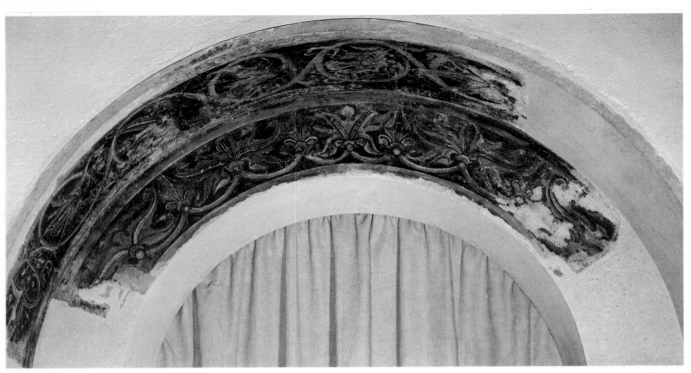

walls virtually nothing) had lost their colour, almost without exception. And so what was perhaps the greatest series of early thirteenth-century paintings anywhere in Europe had been wrecked beyond repair.

But the paintings had also been seen, before the disaster, by Dr Ainau, at present Director of the Museum of Catalan Art in Barcelona. He and Gudiol together arranged for such fragments of painted plaster as had survived to be collected, brought to Barcelona, and eventually pieced together and permanently exhibited, as it were *in situ*, in a room built to the pattern of the original Chapter House. Dr Ainau, studying the techniques of Romanesque wall paintings and their conservation, is still not without some hope that ways will eventually be found by some brilliant new laboratory method to restore, partially at least, some of the original colour. What survives now, to preserve a permanent record of that colour, is a small painted side-arch, no doubt once over a door (Ill.3), where the fine patterned decoration somehow escaped the effects of the fire, perhaps because a fall of masonry protected it.

Some of Gudiol's magnificent photographs were published in 1940, and after the war of 1939–45, the book in which they appeared came into the hands of Professor Otto Pächt. He recognised at once not only that the paintings were English, but that they must be closely connected with the later generation of artists who worked on the illustrations in the huge twelfth-century Bible now in the Winchester Cathedral library, and no doubt made for the Priory of St Swithun. One of these was named, in a study of the various illuminations of the Bible which had appeared a few years before his discovery,[1] *The Master of the Morgan Leaf*; so called, because he also painted the two sides of a splendidly illuminated leaf—evidently made for the Winchester Bible, though not it seems ever bound into it—that now belongs to the Morgan Library in New York. This was the artist whose style Dr Pächt particularly connected with the Sigena paintings. We are here concerned to examine further this remarkable discovery, which he made known in an article, now famous, in the *Burlington Magazine*;[2] to examine also the relationship of these paintings (a relationship to which he alludes) to the Sicilian Mosaics, which were perhaps the finest, certainly the richest, works of decorative art made in Europe in the twelfth century.

The Sigena Wall Paintings

The Chapter House was a large rectangular hall, spanned by five arches. Paintings covered not only the four walls, but also the spandrels of all five arches, on each face: that is to say, four spandrels to each of the arches; the soffits of the arches being painted also. The paintings on these arches were never whitewashed; and, all things considered, the amount of restoration they had suffered was small. Nothing indeed in the way of restoration can be detected in the main area of painting on the arches. It was at the lower corners, where the work was easily accessible, that some repainting, both on the spandrels, and on the soffits had been done. The lower part of the painting of *Moses receiving the Tablets of the Law*, for instance (Ills.44 and 46), had been extensively tampered with, as had the soffit adjacent to it where the later work has a seventeenth-century look. The reason may have been damage to the soffit painting by water, which has certainly wrought havoc at some time with the paintings on the other face of this arch (Ill.51) though there the restorers left the original paintings untouched. There is no trace of the later restorations in the existing fragments now in Barcelona; these coarse fragments having been left in their place on the damaged arches, where they can still be seen. For a reason that is not obvious the heads on the soffits of the arches (Ills.73–126) survived much better than did the more important paintings on the spandrels. On one or two of these 'portraits' on the soffits, some colour is still visible, whereas elsewhere save on the small side arch mentioned, there is now virtually no trace of it. One of these portraits now rephotographed for the purpose, is reproduced as the frontispiece to this book. It gives some idea of the colour plan of the original, though it is only a pale echo of what it was, as the painted decoration of the doorway arch remains to show.

Nothing whatever survived the fire from the Nativity series on the west wall, which certainly contained some of the finest work in the building. From the opposite end of the room, there are remains of the *Crucifixion* painting. They are difficult to decipher, but to some extent supplement the photographs, which show much of the wall still covered with whitewash. One can now see, for instance, behind the cross, an architectural landscape. Flanking the main theme, there was a *Flagellation* on one side, and an *Entombment* on the other. These, and indeed all the paintings (except, as already mentioned, one or two small sections on the soffits of the arches) look today as if they had been executed in a sort of

11

Annunciation
to the Virgin

Visitation

Nativity

Annunciation
to the Shepherds

Creation of Eve

Creation of Adam

Forbidding of the Tree of Knowledge

Adam sleeping—Temptation of Eve

Presentation
in the Temple

Angel teaching Adam to dig

Expulsion from Paradise

Adam digs—Eve spins

Offerings of Cain and Abel

Temptation

Building of the Ark

Cain killing Abel

Noah embarks the Animals

Dove returning to the Ark

Sacrifice of Isaac

Drunkenness of Noah

Pharaoh overwhelmed in the Red Sea

Moses and Aaron, pointing to the Pillar of Fire

Christ in Limbo
(? or elsewhere on
this side of the room)

Raising of Lazarus

Worship of the Golden Calf

Giving of the Law

Anointing of David

Moses striking the Rock

Entombment

Crucifixion

Flagellation

4 and 5. Interior of the Chapter House at Sigena before its destruction

grisaille: or rather in a scheme of dark browns and black, against a brown background. This effect is caused, it would seem, not by the burning off of the surface paint, so that the underpainting is left; but rather by a process in which the surface paint, though losing its colour, has to some extent been fused with the surface plaster. Thus what is visible now is not the original veneda (dark grey) which survives in some English examples[3] because it was painted on a wetted plaster, as an undercoat, and now, with the finishing paint no longer there, gives the odd impression of a photographic negative image. That was not, so far as can be judged, the technique of these paintings.[4] What we now see is more like the photographic positive image, in which, though the effect is monochrome, yet the drawing and modelling of the surface has to some extent survived and has been permanently stabilised. But the varying intensity of the heat certainly affected different areas differently, for, as mentioned above, in one or two small sections some surface colour actually remains.

The general lay-out of the room with its decoration can be seen in Ills.4 and 5 showing the Chapter House before its destruction, and is best explained by reference to the diagram. The spandrels of all the arches were decorated with scenes from the Old Testament. On the first arch, facing outwards towards the New Testament scenes on the west wall (at this end were the *Annunciation* [Ill.54], the *Nativity* [Ill.53], and the *Annunciation to the Shepherds* [Ill.60]) were the *Creation of Adam*, right (Ill.11) and of *Eve*, left (Ill.10). There are no photographs of these particular spandrels as a whole, only of the details; no doubt because when the photographs were taken the lenses available would have needed to be set farther away from their subjects than the position of the end walls allowed. To compare

8. Fragments of the Sigena Wall paintings, as reconstructed in the Museum of Catalan Art, Barcelona

these paintings with the mosaics, almost contemporary with them at Palermo and Monreale, is to notice at once the absence of those *Creation of the Universe* scenes for which the patrons who planned decorations in those semi-Byzantine Christian churches asked. Such scenes occur for example in the Palatina Chapel in Palermo, and in the Cathedral at Monreale, buildings which are both only a generation or so earlier than the Sigena paintings, and the mosaics in one of which at any rate certainly influenced the artists who made those paintings, in ways that will be discussed later. In each of these two Sicilian churches, six scenes, with variations between the two series, followed by a representation of the *Sabbath Day's Rest*, were included. These were all omitted from the Sigena programme. Thus at Sigena the *Fall of Man* rather than the *Creation of the World* emerges as the theme of the Old Testament series. It leads up to the anointing of David as King—a painting which faces that of the *Crucifixion* of the Lord's Anointed, 'great David's greater son' and it is illustrated in considerably more detail than at Monreale or at Palermo. So on the other face of the first arch, the *Forbidding of the Tree of Knowledge* is on one half (Ill.12) and the *Temptation of Eve* (Ill.13) while Adam sleeps, on the other. On the second arch came the *Expulsion from Paradise* (Ill.14) with the *Angel teaching Adam to dig* (Ill.15) in the other spandrel. On the reverse of this arch are *Adam digging and Eve spinning* (Ill.23) in one spandrel, in the other the *Offerings of Cain and Abel* (Ill.24). Confronting these on the third arch are the *Killing of Abel by Cain* (Ill.25) and *Noah building the Ark* (Ill.26); and on the reverse of this arch, on one half *Noah sending the Animals into the Ark* (Ill.34), on the other the *Return of the Dove* (Ill.35) with the sprig of olive. On the next arch, the fourth as we move through the room, is the *Drunkenness of Noah* (Ill.36), and, in the other spandrel of this side, the *Sacrifice of Isaac* (Ill.37). The spandrels on the reverse face show *Moses with Aaron pointing to the Pillar of Fire* (Ill.39), and *Pharaoh's chariots overwhelmed in the Red Sea* (Ill.38). The fifth arch has on the first face, the *Giving of the Law to Moses* (Ill.44), and the *Worship*

9. Carved and painted wooden ceiling from the Sigena Chapter House

16

of the Golden Calf (Ill.45); the subjects on the other face being *Moses striking the Rock* (Ill.51) and the *Anointing of David* (Ill.52). As mentioned already, this arch (particularly on the second side), has suffered from water damage. Facing this fifth arch on the end wall were the *Flagellation, Crucifixion* and *Entombment,* (Ills.64, 66, 67). On the side walls, also, as on both end walls, the paintings were New Testament subjects, and one of these, the *Presentation in the Temple* (Ill.62) which came between the first and second arches on the right side, was among the best preserved of all; though like many of the New Testament series, it had had its surface pitted with the point of a pick as a preliminary no doubt to some intended new plastering and new scheme of decoration, which in the event was not carried out. Next to it came what was apparently a representation of two of the *Temptations,* the scrolls in Christ's hands doubtless carrying his answer to the Devil—a picture over which a portrait probably of the royal Foundress of the Convent seems normally to have hung in later times; and next to that came the *Raising of Lazarus* (Ill.63), also concealed in later times, and no doubt damaged, by the hanging of a portrait over it. Another photograph shows what was apparently *Christ in Limbo* (Ill.71). It is difficult to place precisely. The walls and arches were lit by a series of small windows, one between each pair of arches, on the left-hand side as the viewer stood facing the Nativity-pictures end of the room.

One further element in the general scheme was the series of portrait busts on the soffits of the five arches (Ills.73–126). These are in rectangular frames, arranged arch by arch one above the other; seven portraits on each side up to the point of the arch. The subjects are a single individual in one series; but the father represented with his son in the other.

The portraits nearest ground level seem often to have been in worse condition —or perhaps merely from their position were readier victims for the restorer. Certainly a number were insensitively repainted, inscriptions and all, at a later date, and this later work is obvious in the photographs.

Old & New Testament Scenes

10. Creation of Eve

11. Creation of Adam

Next two pages—above 12–13. Forbidding of the Tree of Knowledge; Adam sleeping; Temptation of Eve

below 14–15. Expulsion from Paradise; Angel teaching Adam to dig

16. God, the Father. Detail of 12

17. Adam sleeping. Detail of 13

18 and 19.   Animals from the Expulsion from Paradise. Detail of 14

21. Angel digging. Detail of 15

22. Eve spinning. Detail of 23

Next two pages—above 23–24. Eve spinning and Adam toiling; Offerings of Cain and Abel

below 25–26. Cain killing Abel; Noah building the Ark

27–29. Foliage and Animal Ornaments. Details of 23, 24, 25

30. Cain. Detail of 25

31.   Abel. Detail of 25

32. Adam digging. Detail of 23

33. Noah building the Ark. Detail of 26

34. Noah sending the Animals into the Ark

35. The Return of the Dove

Next two pages—above 36–37. Drunkenness of Noah; Sacrifice of Isaac

below 38–39. Pharaoh's Chariots overwhelmed in the Red Sea; Moses and Aaron pointing to the Pillar of Fire

40. Noah drunk. Detail of 36

41. Moses and Aaron. Detail of 39

43 (above). Fighting Centaur. Detail of 39

42 (left). Lion. Detail of 36

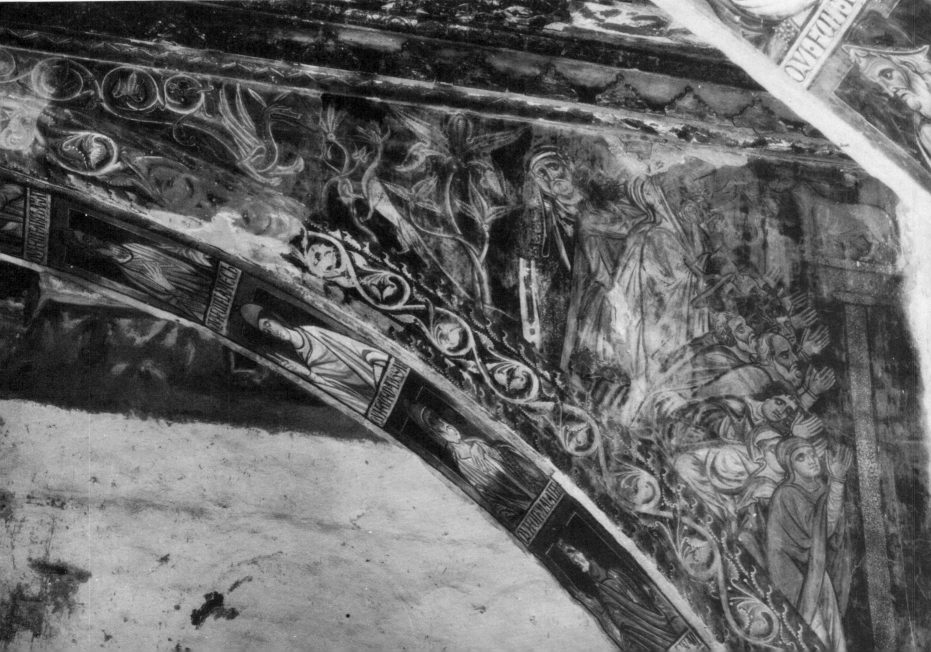

46. Moses receiving the Law. Detail of 44
(Lower part of the figure of Moses modern)

44 (left above). Giving of the Law

45 (left below). Worship of the Golden Calf

49. Goats. Detail of 48

Previous two pages—left 47. Israelites worshipping

right 48. David's Flocks

50. Drolleries

51. Moses striking the Rock

52. Anointing of David

53. Nativity

55. Visitation

54. Annunciation

56. Detail of 53

57. Detail of 53

58. Head of Joseph. Detail of 53

59. Head of Mary. Detail of 53

60. Annunciation to the Shepherds

61. Detail of 60

62. Presentation in the Temple

63 (right above). Raising of Lazarus

64 (right below). Flagellation (newly photographed in the Museum of Catalan Art, Barcelona)

67.   Fragment from the Entombment (newly photographed in the Museum of Catalan Art, Barcelona)

65 (left above). Angel above the Crucifixion (newly photographed in the Museum of Catalan Art, Barcelona)

66 (left below).   Crucifixion

71. Christ in Limbo

72. Harrowing of Hell

73-90.   Ancestors of Christ. Portraits on the Soffits of the Arches

91–126. Ancestors of Christ. Portraits on the Soffits of the Arches

109

QVI·FVIT·ELIEZER

113

QVI·FVIT·ELIACHIM

117

QVI·FVIT·OBED

122

QVI·FVIT·NOE

110

QVI·FVIT·IORAM·

114

QVI·FVIT·NATHAN

118

QVI·FVIT·ABRAHE

123

QVI·FVIT·SEM

111

QVI·FVIT·SYMEON

115

QVI·FVIT·DAVID

119

QVI·FVIT·SAAC

124

QVI·FVIT·CAYNAN

112

VI·FVIT·IONA·

116

QVI·FVIT·IESSE

120

QVI·FVIT·IACOB

125

QVI·FVIT·GNOS

Next two pages—127. Aminadab;   128. Naasson. Soffit portraits

121

QVI·FVIT·ARPHAXAT

126

QVI·FVIT·SETH

AMINADAB.Q.NEAS

NAERSON·A·GEH·SALOMÕ

The Genealogy Portrait Series

The arrangement of the portraits was on five arches; the two at the *Nativity* end of the building contained the Matthaean genealogy, with the formula in the inscriptions *'autem genuit'* (both words being normally abbreviated), and with the portraits showing both father and son; in the Lucan series, on the remaining three arches, the formula was *'qui fuit'* and each portrait represented only one person.

The Matthaean genealogy displays the descent only from Abraham: in the Gospel this represents forty generations; but each arch had only seven portraits on each soffit, so that, on two arches, there were only twenty-eight places, and the genealogy had to be correspondingly shortened—simply by omissions here and there. The earliest part of the genealogy was on the first arch, adjacent, that is, to the *Nativity* wall.

The Lucan genealogy displays the descent from Adam. This amounts, in the original, to seventy-five generations.

Three arches allowed only forty-two places; so that once again the genealogy had to be drastically shortened. The earliest part of the genealogy here was on the fifth arch, i.e. that next to the wall with the *Crucifixion* painting.

Apart from the omissions, there is at least one variation of order to be seen in the surviving photographs: on the crown of the fifth arch (in the early part of the Lucan series, that is) the order of the paintings is Shem, Noah, Arphaxath, which is not as in the biblical text. The artist's practice was to continue the order through the crown of the arch; starting at the foot of the soffit, he ran the series up to the crown, and then down the other side. The series of portraits on the five arches amounted originally to seventy (five arches with fourteen portraits on each). Many are not represented in the series of photographs that has survived; and many of the portraits at the foot of the arches on either side had been completely repainted.

MATTHEW (formula 'autem genuit') Ills. 73–93

Abraham	*Booz	Ozias	*Abiud
Isaac	*Obed	Ioathan	*Eliacim
Jacob	*Iesse	Achaz	*Azor
Juda	*David	Ezecias	*Sadoc
*Phares	*Salomon	Manasses	Achim
*Esron	*Roboam	*Amon	Eliud
*Aram	Abia	*Iosias	Eleazar
*Aminadab	Asa	*Iechonias	Mathan
*Naasson	Josaphat	*Salathiel	Jacob
*Salmon	Ioram	*Zorobabel	Joseph

LUKE (formula 'qui fuit') Ills. 94–126

Joseph	Zorobabel	Menna	Sarug
Heli	Salathiel	Matthatha	Ragau
Matthat	Neri	*Nathan	Phaleg
Levi	Melchi	*David	Heber
*Melchi	Addi	*Jesse	Sale
*Ianne	Cosam	*Obed	Cainan
*Joseph	*Elmadan	Booz	*Arphaxad
*Matthathias	*Her	Salmon	*Sem
*Amos	*Iesu	Naasson	*Noe
*Naum	*Eliezer	Aminadab	Lamech
Hesli	*Iorim	Aram	Mathusale
*Nagge	Matthat	Esron	Henoch
Mahath	Levi	Phares	Iared
Matthathias	*Simeon	Judas	Malaleel
*Semei	Iuda	*Jacob	*Cainan
*Joseph	Joseph	*Isaac	*Henos
*Juda	*Iona	*Abraham	*Seth
*Iohanna	*Eliacim	Thare	Adam
*Resa	Melcha	Nachor	

* Included in the Portrait Series and reproduced

Byzantinism at Sigena

The powerful Byzantinising of the Sigena paintings had been observed before Pächt identified them as English. It is therefore necessary to consider in general what Byzantine sources had already contributed to English twelfth-century art in order to assess the peculiarly Byzantine characteristics of this particular group of paintings; and then to discover, if it can be done, the special sources these artists had for this inspiration. The interest of the Sigena series lies at least partly in the fact that they belong to a period, or perhaps rather a critical moment, of changing fashion. It comes at a time when English art had begun to move away, under the impact of fresh Byzantine ideas, from the conventions of the Romanesque manner. Byzantine art itself was revitalised, again and again during its history, by classical revivals: by a renewed study of the antique for which there were materials available in Constantinople and the Eastern Empire, which were taken more seriously than similar materials in Italy. The taste for a high degree of formalism, such as is seen (to quote an early, mid-ninth-century example) in the almost fantastic mosaic representing the Ascension in the dome at Salonica (Ill.129), with its strained, stilted, extravagantly tall figures, changes, perhaps within the same century, towards a new naturalism as in the paintings at Castel Seprio[5] in northern Italy (Ill.130). This phase turns out, however, to be not so much new as a revival of the classical tradition and its techniques. The same thing can be seen happening in the twelfth century, and, here again, the two fashions seem to be followed almost side by side: the one does not supersede the other. Thus there is a fine group of paintings in the little church at Asinou in Cyprus, exactly datable to the first decade of the century, which in fact seems to have been executed some years later than the most classicising of the mosaics at Daphni near Athens—mosaics of exceptional quality, for which classical models seem to have been followed at first hand, and which show their classical derivation in a number of ways. The most obvious is in the stance of the figures (Ill.132). The weight now seems to be distributed naturally, whereas before the pose had been determined by an interest, as in the *Ascension* mosaic at Salonica, in dramatic contortion (Ill.131). This contortion was sometimes intended to express an emotion like grief or anger (in that example, the spellbound surprise of the apostles, beings in themselves almost infinitely removed—as they are so often in Byzantine art—from the ordinary); at other times, it seems simply to have been a manifestation of the artist's interest in pattern. By contrast, the Daphni figure stands like a human being. The classical 'vision' there manifests itself also, most markedly, in the way draperies are observed: the folds begin, in the

129.   Ascension. Mosaic, mid 9th century. Salonica, St Sophia

130.   Detail from the Flight into Egypt. Wall-painting, 9th century (?). Castel Seprio, Italy   131.   Detail of 129

132 (above). Prophets. Mosaic, end of 11th century. Daphni, Monastery

133. Death of the Virgin. Painting, 1105–6. Asinou, Church of Our Lady

classical style, to be represented as they might be if copied from the actual material, and the high-lights begin to gleam erratically, while in the other, the folds were organised—even regimented—into patterns taking no notice of the force of gravity, planned, once again, as part of a larger formalised scheme in which the high-lights themselves become extremely delicate formal designs, as if worked like a damask into the fabric.

The paintings at Asinou still show, in contrast to the Daphni mosaics, much of the preoccupation with pattern, rather than with nature. In the *Death of the Virgin* which is here illustrated (Ill.133), the most elegant hairdresser could hardly hope to create the formal curls which cover the head of St Peter. The cloak and skirt on the dead body of the Virgin do not hang over it but are drawn towards the foot like the flutings of a fallen column. There is a brilliant counterpoint in the attitudes of the mourners. But even there, what we feel is the repeatedly self-conscious behaviour of each group in order to elaborate the general pattern. Particularly in the paler draperies, the artist is absorbed in the interest of sweeping curves and oval shapes, which bear no relation to the natural fall of woven materials.

77

134. St Paul. Mosaic, second half of 12th century. Palermo, Cappella Palatina

135. St Paul. Detail of Wall painting, mid-12th century. Canterbury Cathedral

These two very different fashions, the formal and the naturalistic, thus manifest themselves almost simultaneously in twelfth-century Byzantine art. But the classicising style is less usual (at any rate in provincial paintings) than the pattern development, more subtle, perhaps more difficult to assimilate in default of actual classical models which were comparatively few and far between; while the other style appealed more markedly to those brought up in the Romanesque tradition in the west, which started, so to say, with much in common with it. The classicising movement is so shy in its emergence that E. Kitzinger, in a well-known article,[6] spoke in regard to it of 'parallelisms' rather than influences: of developments that took place at the same time in different regions, because they belonged ultimately to the same tradition—but which were not directly connected with one another. We shall ourselves incline rather to the view that our Sigena painters had had some direct experience of mosaics and paintings done by Byzantine artists in the classical manner; and that it is realistic to talk of both fashions affecting English twelfth-century art, directly and profoundly, the pattern interest however appearing several generations before the other.

If we take as an example (from the mid-twelfth century) the great Canterbury wall painting of St Paul (Ill.135), there are to be seen in it clear indications of such Byzantine pattern-structures. The saint is shown leaning forward to shake the viper from his hand into the fire, in an attitude certainly derived from a Byzantine model. It is close to, but actually less exaggerated than, the *St Paul of the Damascus Road Conversion*, shown temporarily blinded and helpless, in the Cappella Palatina at Palermo (Ill.134). The face, hands and feet are in fact delicately modelled, and show the beginnings of what is, in England, the later fashion. But the drapery, a most beautiful achievement, is elaborately organised in a wonderful series of folds that have nothing to do with what would be seen on an actual

78

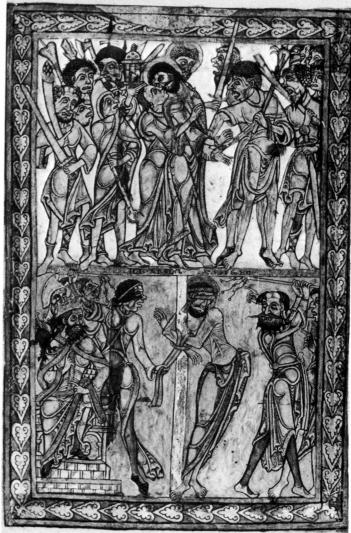

136 and 137. Winchester Psalter Miniatures: Virgin Orans, fol. 27r; Flagellation, fol. 21r. London, British Museum, Cotton Ms Nero C IV

model. The cloak over the left arm does not fall from the wrist, but scoops back in an artificial curve enriched by fine but quite unrealistic detail on the inside as well as the outside. On the right side of the body, and over the thigh and calf, the high-lights show as if they were woven damask arabesques. Over the right arm, the sleeve of the white tunic picks up the oval motif which we saw in the Asinou painting from Cyprus, made (we remind ourselves) in the early years of the century. We saw there also the solid regular folds recurring here, there and everywhere to give the basic sense of pattern to the whole. The effect is so fine in the Canterbury example that we bother no more than did the artist about the difficulties of any fabric assuming these shapes in nature. Many French manuscripts, and many English manuscripts also, derive their original inspiration from models like the Asinou *Death of the Virgin*. A splendid example is the Bible from Bury St Edmunds (e.g. fol. 94) of which a fragment is now in Cambridge. In it the balance between the older fashion and the new is held at almost precisely the same point as it is in the St Paul. By contrast, the artist of a *Flagellation* (Ill.137), in a Psalter from Winchester (which is no doubt close in date to the Canterbury *St Paul*), like others working in the Romanesque tradition, seized on these pattern schemes and exaggerated them more uncompromisingly, more forcefully, and more dramatically, than they appear in any Byzantine examples. Here the face of the suffering figure is impassive; those of the mockers are caricatures. But the contorted body conveys intensely the agony of the ordeal and its tension. It is about as far removed from any classical interpretation as it could be.

Paradoxically, however, there is in that same Winchester Psalter a pair of paintings in an idiom stylistically and iconographically so notably Byzantine, that according to Professor Wormald[7] they were sometimes considered the work of an Italo-Byzantine artist. He pointed to several characteristics that stamp them nevertheless definitely as English work, though evidently done under powerful Byzantine inspiration. In them the beginnings of the classical revival can be seen. The signs of it are in the comparatively easy, natural stance of the archangels on either side of the Virgin (Ill.136); in the slight lean of the heads which enhances further the sense of ease; and, above all, the high degree of modelling in hands and faces, which have here become three dimensional. Nothing seems to have survived in other books in this hand. In the Winchester Bible, the great exponent of the Byzantine manner[8] is the Master of the Morgan Leaf, whose style is not only more masterly but shows far more individualisation—one face being always markedly different from another; it is a style too in which the clothes hang far more naturally. The Virgin's dress in the Psalter painting is still, after all, highly formal, as is seen in the long sharp creases with their arrowhead ends, or the charming arabesques that do duty for high-lights. In this picture, then, the classical manner has travelled only half the distance towards the transformation that will be seen in the Sigena paintings.

The full development of the new style in the Bible is shown perhaps most strikingly in a sketch (Ill.138) for two initials side by side, initials for two versions of the same psalm. (Throughout this particular book of the Bible, these double initials recur.) The artist seems to have been a colleague of the Master of the Morgan Leaf, and has been named the Master of the Gothic Majesty.[9] His sketch, because it is so highly simplified, gives the essentials of the new fashion in a way that his completed painting, elsewhere in the Bible, does not. The four figures, seated so easily and naturally, the delicately indicated and thoroughly naturalistic fall of skirts and mantles, are an extraordinary contrast to the same subject (Ill.139) as treated by one of the earlier Romanesque masters in the Bible, the Master of the Leaping Figures. In this earlier treatment, the uneasy Monarch can hardly be said either to sit or to stand. His strange contorted attitude betokens neither with any certainty. There can hardly be more than a decade or so between the earlier and the later. The Master of the Leaping Figures' initial occurs in the second half of the Bible and cannot have been done till a comparatively late stage in the writing of the work. But with its fierce colours, as well as with its design conceived in terms of pattern, it sums up the characteristics of the early style, as the sketches do of the later.

Here is to be noted again, however, a point observed already: that the earlier styles themselves owed debts, though of a different kind, to Byzantine models. Peter's head tightly massed with curls was noticed earlier in the Asinou painting (Ill.133). The heads drawn by the Master of the Leaping Figures are often similarly covered with a pattern of curls, undoubtedly Byzantine in origin. The debt is also often iconographical. The two initials side by side at the opening of the Book of Psalms, for instance, designed (though not painted) by the Master of the Leaping Figures, and showing the young David leaping on to the backs of the lion and bear to protect his flock (Ill.141), adapt a late classical design which the Master is likely to have found in some Byzantine work. The intermediary in this instance may have been a fabric like the silk in the Victoria and Albert Museum (Ill.140) into which such a design is woven. But the Byzantinising of the earlier

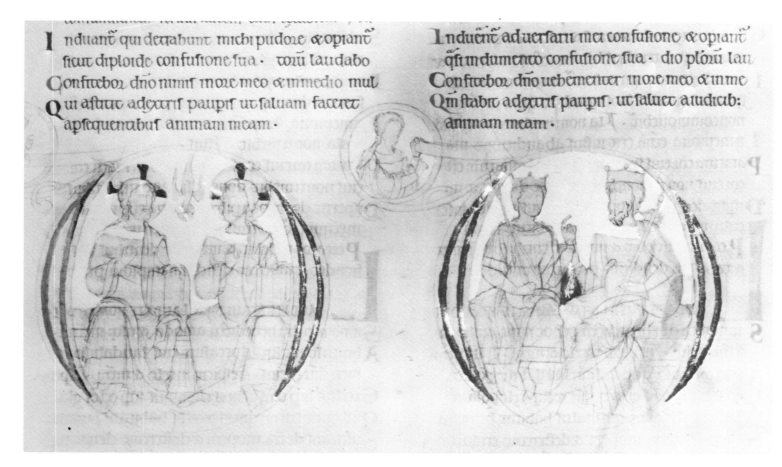

Induent qui detrahunt michi pudore & opiant
sicut diploide confusione sua · tou̅ laudabo
Confitebor dn̅o nimis more meo & in medio mul
Qui astitit adextris paupis ut saluam faceret
apsequentibus animam meam ·

Induent aduersarii mei confusione & opiant
qsi indumento confusione sua · dio plou̅ lau
Confitebor dn̅o uehementer in ore meo & in me
Qm̅ stabit adextris paupis · ut saluet a iudicib:
animam meam ·

138. Unfinished Initial by the Master of the Gothic Majesty. Winchester Bible, fol. 250r

139. Initial by the Master of the Leaping Figures. Winchester Bible, fol. 270

140. Byzantine Silk, c. 8th century.
London, Victoria and Albert Museum

141. Opening Initial to the Book of Psalms.
Winchester Bible, fol. 218r

masters is very different from the 'classicising' Byzantinism of the later. And it is this which now demands our attention, particularly in the work of the Master of the Morgan Leaf and the Master of the Gothic Majesty.

An unexpected feature of the Winchester Bible is this fact just mentioned in connection with the opening pair of initials to the Book of Psalms that in a number of initials the final painting is the work of a different Master from the designer.[10] In more than one instance, as with another of the Psalms initials (Ill.159), the painting was never completed, and there are still areas in which the original design, here unmistakably in the hand of the Leaping Figures Master (though the Morgan Leaf Master is the painter), still shows. And, as it happened, the technique of all these illuminators was to complete first (once the actual design was ready) any areas intended to be overlaid with gold. All of them observed this sequence: design; gilding; painting. But the use they made of gold, differed greatly. We shall see reason to think that some of the later masters had seen some of the Sicilian mosaics, themselves made about this time. Perhaps, from seeing the gold backgrounds of these mosaics, these later masters developed their practice of using gold as the background to the initial, the figures being as it were silhouetted boldly against its dazzling brilliance. The early Master of the Leaping Figures did no such thing. In his work, narrow strips of gold, seldom more than 4 mm broad, outline initials; and still narrower edges of gold provide a rich fringe to many of the garments on the figures he designs and paints. Half a dozen initials designed by him exist,[11] in the unfinished second half of the Bible, in which he had drawn out his design, and laid on the gold where he wanted it, but in which he has taken matters no further. It is manifest that another artist, whose habit was to use gold in a different way, but who took over a half-finished design so treated, would find his style inevitably modified by the need to follow, in the designs of the clothes, the lines laid down by these golden fringes. To have scrapped the gold would have been not only difficult but costly. So he did what he could within the lines already laid down by the gold edges. Precisely this has happened in the initials shown in Ills.141 and 143.

It is now possible to say with confidence that the Morgan Leaf itself, from which the Morgan Master takes his name, is an instance of work designed in one hand and painted in another; and that this applies to both sides of the leaf. It is also possible to show that the original design on both sides is in the hand of the artist known as the Master of the Apocrypha drawings—the name derived from two full pages of drawings (these two, however, unlike the Morgan Leaf never painted) in the unfinished second half of the Bible (see Ill.142). The story, pieced together from bibliographical as well as stylistic evidence, seems to be that when the actual writing of the Winchester Bible had passed beyond the half-way mark, and a number of initials (but not yet nearly all), in the part so far written, had been designed and painted, a decision was taken to make the book even more splendid by including in it some full pages of decoration, such as already embellished others of the great Bibles of the period. At least one[12] such further decoration was planned to be added to the part already written—none of which, we may be certain, had yet been bound up into book form. It was to stand before

142. Full-page drawing for Maccabees by the Master of the Apocrypha Drawings. Winchester Bible, fol. 350v

the 'First Book of Kings' (I Samuel as it is now called) and the subjects illustrated were to be from the lives of Samuel, Saul and David. It was necessary to duplicate a half-column of chapter headings to ensure that the text of these was completed immediately following the first half of the series (the first written, of the pair which duplicate one another, would have no doubt been erased, with pumice, if the plan had ever been carried through); and because there was already an initial drawing (by the Master of the Leaping Figures) to I Kings, showing Elkanah sitting at meat with his wives (Ill.143), the designer of the full-page decorations avoided this particular theme—which his work was planned to supplement—and treated, mainly, later elements in the story.

This designer, the Master of the Apocrypha Drawings, did not, it seems, belong to Winchester. His hand was recognised, many years ago, in a remarkable

143. Initial to I Kings. Winchester Bible, fol. 88r

manuscript that belonged originally to St Albans;[13] and Professor Wormald has rightly pointed out the close connection of some of the work done on the Winchester Bible, by him or his assistants, with earlier paintings for St Albans. When he gave up his work on the Bible, he left behind the two full pages of drawings which are now bound up in the second volume of the Bible; and evidently left also the two sides of drawings on the Morgan Leaf, not yet painted either—in addition to five initials completed and one not yet completed in his style.

The task of painting these designs of the 'I Kings' decorated pages (the Morgan Leaf), and also the initial at the beginning of 'I Kings' which would go with them, was assigned eventually to another artist, who seems similarly to have been a visitor to Winchester rather than brought up in the Winchester tradition. He had already, it seems, travelled far afield, if the judgement (later to be examined in more detail) that he had already seen the Sicilian mosaics of Cefalù Cathedral, and of the Cappella Palatina in Palermo, is right. Certainly he already worked confidently in the new Byzantine classical style. His individualising of the personages he represents is without parallel in English illumination of his day. The modelling of the faces he draws is to an extraordinary degree three-dimensional, compared with the work of his English predecessors. And, when he himself designs what he later paints, the clothes are represented as hanging naturally on the body. In painting both the Morgan Leaf, however, and the initial to 'I Kings', he was working over designs in the Romanesque style. Especially on the *recto* of the leaf, evidently the first side he painted, he was for some reason (perhaps the instructions of the patron, whoever that was, who planned the book) following these much more closely. Compare for instance the clothes of the young bearer of one of the offerings in the *Presentation* scene on the *recto* (Ill.144)—the tunic fitting so tightly over the body, and the stiffly designed kilt, its formal fold springing from the bunching material at the waist—with those of the young David on the *verso* of the leaf (Ill.145), where he is shown swinging his sling to let fly the stone at Goliath. The former figure, very beautiful indeed, is nevertheless stilted in pose, and the clothes are highly formalised.

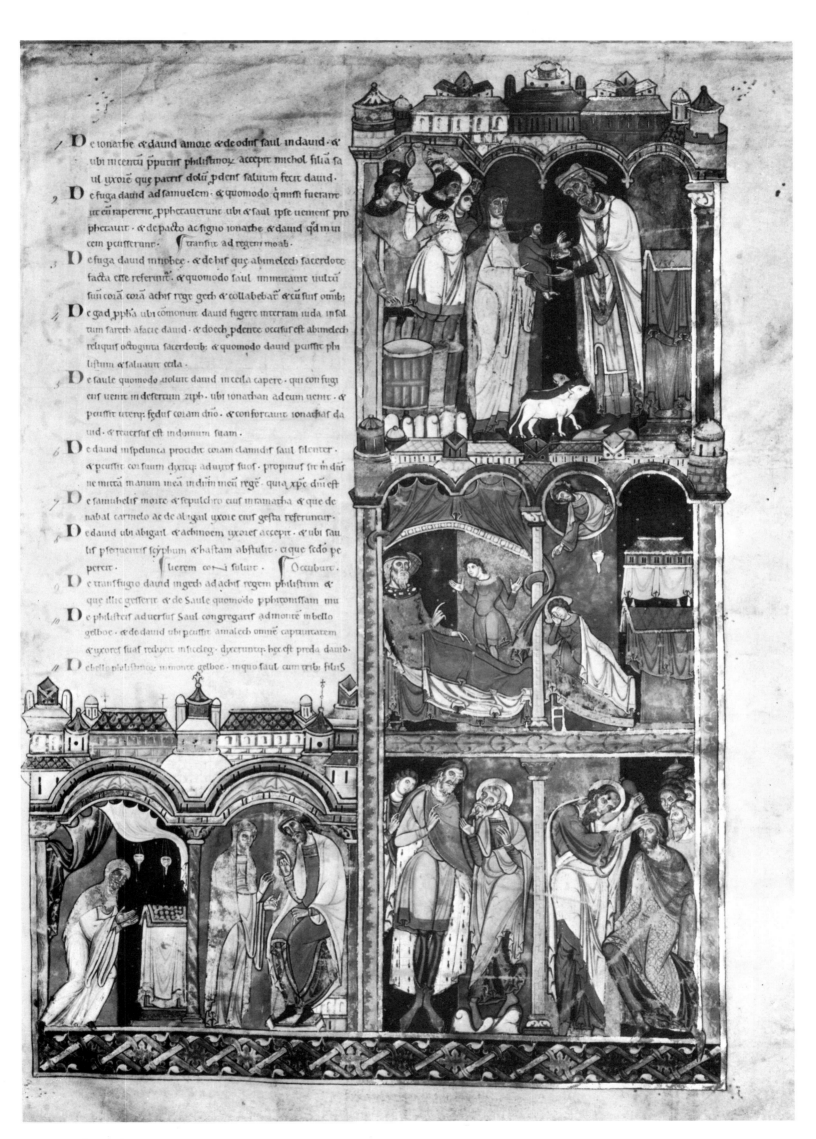

144. Story of Samuel. Detached page. New York, Pierpont Morgan Library, Ms. 619 recto

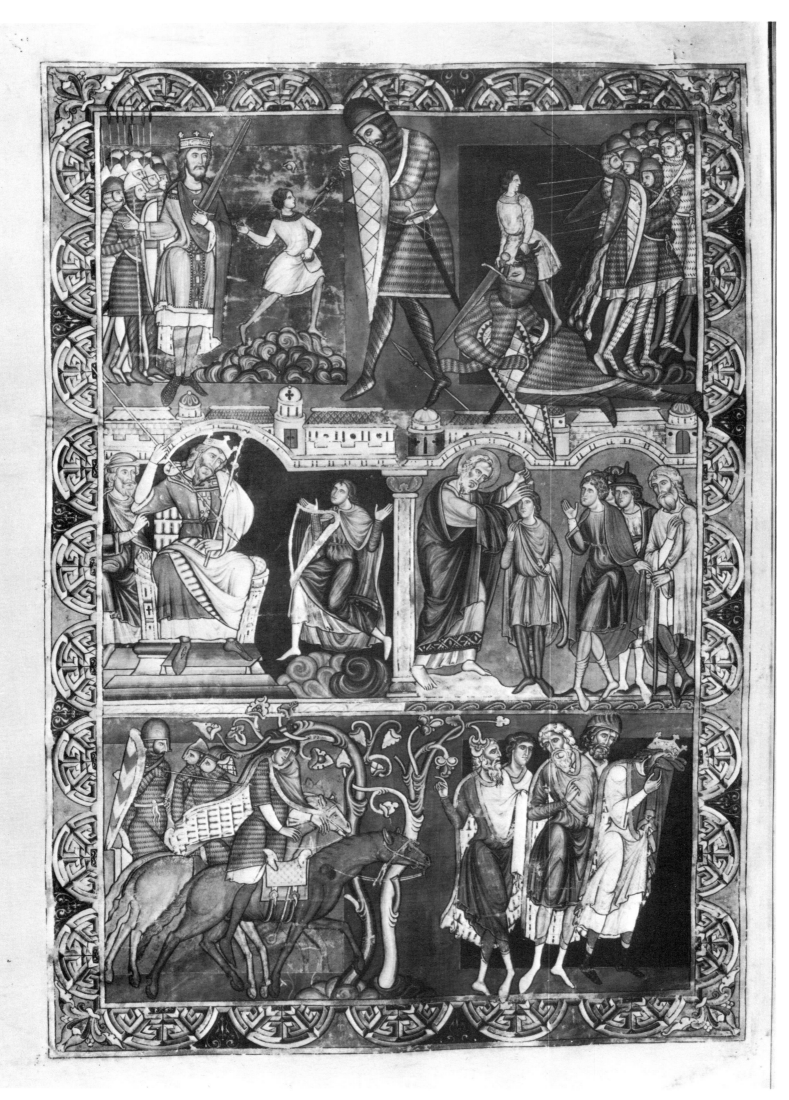

145.   Story of David. Verso of 144. New York, Pierpont Morgan Library, Ms. 619 verso

The second has an easy freedom about him; the fall of the tunic and kilt is loose and natural. Or compare the skirt of Eli in the lower register on the *recto* and particularly the series of folds within the major fold, forming a 'ruffle' design of tight loops climbing upwards,[14] with the skirts worn by David and his courtiers on the *verso*, hanging so much more naturally. It might be tempting to assume that different artists painted the two sides of the leaf. Yet, throughout both sides, we see already something always characteristic of his work; modified indeed, but still as I shall suggest recognisable, much later, at Sigena: those faces not only with a remarkable degree of modelling and of characterisation, but with their grave and sad dignity, the older contrasting so powerfully with the fresh, sometimes almost smug, self-confidence of the more youthful. We are concerned undoubtedly on both sides of the leaf with a single personality as the painter. Alternatively, we might perhaps have supposed that the designer of the *verso* was different from the designer of the *recto*. But this idea also becomes untenable when it is observed that on both the *verso* and the *recto*, here and there, there has been flaking of the surface paint. In at least two crucial places this flaking shows details of the underdrawing, typically in the style of the Apocrypha Drawings Master. The leaf then, is a composite work; designed, on both sides, by a Romanesque artist, painted on both sides by a man whose sympathies were with a later and very different fashion. And the solemn dignity of the Morgan Leaf period was to become the sombre, almost tragic vision of the later style as we shall observe it at Sigena.

The conclusion that the Morgan Master was not working over his own designs on the Morgan Leaf is of some importance, if we are to use the leaf for comparison. We cannot be sure that any pose or stance on it, is such as he would himself have drawn. Often, indeed by examining on the one hand the original designer's other work (in particular, the two leaves of drawings still in the Winchester Bible) and, on the other, the rest of the Morgan Master's work in the

146. David mourning. Detail of 145   147. Sons of Noah. Detail of 36. Sigena

148. 'Dancer's Stance'. Detail of 142, Maccabees drawing, Winchester Bible

Bible, we can distinguish securely between the parts they played in the work of the leaf itself. That strange stance with the crossed legs—the 'dancer's stance' as Professor Tristram used to call it—is Romanesque, and wholly uncharacteristic of the Morgan Master. We find it often in the Apocrypha Drawings (Ill.148).

149. 'Dancer's Stance'. Detail of Morgan Leaf, 145

The clothes represent an intermediate stage (the progression further on the *verso* of the leaf than on the *recto*) between the tightly fitting garments worn let us say by the Master of the Leaping Figures' *Prophet Jeremiah*, and the loosely worn clothes—evidently classical in their ultimate inspiration—of the Morgan

89

150. Initial to Isaiah. Winchester Bible, fol. 131r

151. Initial to Habakkuk. Winchester Bible, fol. 208r

Master's *Habakkuk* (Ill.151); or of the seated figures in the Gothic Majesty Master's drawing (Ill.138); or of his Almighty in the *Isaiah* initial (Ill.150). But there is no indication that the inner frames of colour, that form so effective a part of the painting on the *verso* of the leaf, come from the Apocrypha Drawings Master's original design. They are part of the contribution the painter made to that splendid work.

Professor Pächt[15] deliberately postponed the question whether the artists of Sigena were actually among those who had worked earlier on the Winchester Bible, or rather some other representatives of the new manner. 'Whether the step from the Master of the Morgan Leaf', he said, 'to the art of Sigena can be viewed as the evolution of a single artistic personality—but after renewed contact with Byzantium—is a question far too complex and delicate to be adequately dealt with in the short space of an article.' And I doubt whether anyone who has studied the work at Sigena closely, with the later work on the Bible, will ever give an absolutely confident answer to this question. We must on general stylistic grounds suppose a gap in time—that could be as long as a couple of decades—between the last Winchester Bible paintings, and Sigena; and these were years not only of changing fashion, but (on any hypothesis which connects the two, and allows also for direct Byzantine influence) of far ranging experience, from the severe, sometimes harsh, Romanesque of Spain to the so much softer, so much more naturalistic, tendencies of the most notable artists then working in the Byzantine tradition. Moreover, we are comparing two widely different media, the miniature with the full-scale. But when I originally discussed these Winchester Bible artists, I said that some (and the Morgan Leaf artist was in my mind) 'seemed to be reaching out beyond the limits of miniature painting to something full-scale'.[16] The initials designed and completed in this Master's

INCIPIT·EZE
CHIEL·PPHETA·
T·
·F·COO·
·E·ST·
IN·TRI
CESIMO

anno·inquarto·inquinta menfif·cum eem inmedio
captuuorum iyxta fluuium chobár·aperti funt
çeli·&uidi uifionef dei·Inquinta menfif·ipfe eft
annuf quintuf transmigrationif regif ioachim·

152.   Initial to Ezekiel. Winchester Bible, fol. 172r

hand are technically as brilliant examples of miniature painting as can be found.
The massy gold background for instance in the *Ezekiel* or *Daniel* initials (Ills.152,
204), is a superlative testimony to the sheer craftsmanship of the miniaturist;
and in this detail at least, the actual craftsmanship is incomparably better than
that shown by the gold in most Byzantine miniatures. But the fact that this man
was technically brilliant in the handling of gold leaf and of parchment does not
in itself exclude the possibility of brilliance in other fields, though it may be
easier to believe in a genius of comparatively narrow, rather than one of exceptionally wide, achievement. And the evidence of such a comprehensive

handbook as that which circulated in the twelfth century under the name of Theophilus (*de diversis artibus*), with the evidence also for the versatility of Master Hugo at Bury St Edmunds about the middle of the century,[17] suggests that artists did not always specialise in one craft only.

The argument in the first place rests on the general impression the paintings give of their Englishness; and there the case has been regarded as unanswerable in Spain as well as elsewhere. It was based originally on a 'stylistic first impression of the physiognomy of the whole'.[18] But it was also supported with a number of detailed observations that were surely conclusive: for instance, the curiously English use by Cain of the jawbone of an ass as his murderous weapon (Ill.30)— whereas continental artists arm him with a club. The fable of the barnacle goose, introduced as a decoration at Sigena next to the representation of *Moses receiving the Law* (Ill.153), is English and not Continental. The fable began in the generation to which the Winchester Bible itself belongs, with the writings of Giraldus Cambrensis, who claims himself to have seen in Ireland the barnacle goose growing from the twigs of a tree. It was then taken up and illustrated in several English bestiaries, but not abroad. The 'octopus' acanthus is primarily English, the 'hallmark of later twelfth-century book ornament in England': the acanthus tendrils 'gripping the coils of the winding scrolls'. This occurs in bold and effective form in the Sigena decorations, and a more delicate version, though the same motif, is developed in the Winchester Bible itself (Ills.154–6). Perhaps most striking of all, the exact key pattern which is used on the *verso* of the Morgan Leaf is used also extensively in the borders of the wall paintings (Ills. 157, 158) at Sigena and, so far as I am aware, known in this precise form only in these two examples. On the paintings of the arches, the bursting Glory is similarly a feature shared by some Winchester painters; a remarkably individual motif, framed in which the divine hand or the face of the Almighty (Ill.44) appears—the same formula being used for the Pillar[19] of Fire (Ill.39).

But Pächt did not go on to assert the identity of the hands; and why not is clear. For the differences between the Master of the Morgan Leaf's style, and that of the Sigena paintings, are unmistakable. The faces at Sigena for example

153. Fable of the Barnacle Goose. Detail of 44, Moses receiving the Law, Sigena

154. Octopus Acanthus Ornament. Initial. Winchester Bible, fol. 204r

155 and 156. Acanthus Ornaments. Sigena

157. Key-pattern Border to Morgan Leaf. Detail of 145

158. Border of Nativity, Sigena

159 (above). Angel. Detail of Winchester Bible Initial, fol. 246r

160 (below). Angel. Detail of 53, Nativity, Sigena

161. Head of Micah. Detail of Winchester Bible Initial, fol. 205r

162. Head of David. Detail of Winchester Bible Initial, fol. 218r

163. Head of Abel. Detail of 24. Sigena

164. Isaiah. Detail of Winchester Bible Initial, fol. 131r

165 (right). Detail of 60, the Annunciation to the Shepherds, Sigena

show, so often, squared corners to the mouth (Ill.163) such as are seen hardly at all in the Winchester Bible, though in the face of David (Ill.162) or of the prophet Micah (Ill.161) the idiom may be beginning. The idiom in which the back of the hand has those curious ridges lifting *between* the bones running to the fingers, not *on* them (a detail perhaps closely observed from the back of the hand held out flat) is at Sigena highly characteristic, while at Winchester it is unknown.[20] Much of the ornament at Sigena is of a character not seen in the Bible: like the fine border design below the *Expulsion from Paradise* (Ill.14), or the elegant lace pattern below the *Sleeping Noah* (Ill.36), or a comparable pattern, again quite unlike Winchester work, below the *Chariot of Pharaoh overwhelmed in the Red Sea* (Ill.38), or the design built up of a bursting pair of fronds, repeated, bordering the scene of *Moses receiving the Law* (Ill.44). But while all these patterns give a different impression from those used in the Bible by this generation of painters, the reason may be largely technical. The artists had seen the jewel-like ornament of some of the Sicilian mosaics; and with gold available they could create similar effects on parchment—as in the ornament of the *Genesis* initial (Ill.180), or the roundel in the *Isaiah* initial with its gold background. This tiny gem-like ornament is not suitable for wall paintings, where, anyhow, gold was not used. It is essentially miniaturistic.

And when the resemblances are examined, they are often so striking that it is hard not to believe in the actual identity of hands. We have already noted the habit of setting the figure work against an inner frame of a different colour from that which edges the painting: the inner colour at Sigena was perhaps a deep blue, as on the *verso* of the Morgan Leaf, where these inner frames are a noteworthy feature. The device is used to focus attention on the figures, in a scheme which, on the spandrels, consists partly of non-figural decorative elements. This had been invented perhaps, certainly used most effectively, by the much earlier St Albans artist of the so-called Hildesheim Psalter.[21] It is used in one initial in the Morgan Leaf Master's hand (*Habakkuk*: Ill.151), actually in the Winchester Bible. At Sigena it was evidently an important element in the Master's plan for the decoration of the Chapter House—whoever the Master responsible was.

And when details are examined, the *Isaiah* initial (Ills.150, 164), evidently one of the latest in the Bible,[22] provides some comparisons with Sigena that seem in themselves almost conclusive. The theme is the Prophet receiving the heavenly message (on a scroll) from the hand of the Almighty. The face is half-lifted, eager; the head is shown wearing a type of hat which certainly occurs elsewhere in English paintings of the period, but duly appears in the Bible, and also in a recently uncovered twelfth-century painting at Winchester (Ill.216). The head, the hat, the eager face are precisely paralleled in one of the Shepherds of the Sigena *Annunciation to the Shepherds* (Ill.165) where he offers a dramatically brilliant contrast with the bucolic air of the other shepherds. The face shows the same rapt attention—this time to the angels' message; and the modelling of the flesh is very close. In the same initial the divine face is similar to the Christ in what seems to have been the *Christ in Limbo* painting at Sigena (Ills.166, 167); and the tree in the background to the initial, to be seen also in miniature in the tailpiece of an initial by this same artist (the Master of the Gothic Majesty) in a

96

Cambridge manuscript,[23] finds its twin in the background of the *Shepherds* painting at Sigena; while the open, looped, acanthus pattern at the top and foot of the stem of the letter seems to be not unlike one of the Sigena borders (Ill.155). The cloudy, conventional ground, beneath the feet of the figures in the initial, has its close and frequent analogies at Sigena (Ills.12,150,151). The similarities in the faces might have been attributed simply to the use of a collection of cartoons—were it not for the particular appropriateness of the expression in both contexts, and to the cumulative evidence of these other details appearing both in the Bible and at Sigena.

Techniques also provide detailed comparative material. One feature to be noted again and again at Sigena on the faces is the high-light, consisting of a disc of white placed just below the eye towards the outer corner, there joined by a line of the same white, that runs under the eye to the edge of the nose and then often downwards, along the inner cheek. At Winchester, precisely the same technique is seen in some initials painted in the later styles. And technical similarities extend to more general points. For some reason not now to be determined, the surface paint in the Sigena *Raising of Lazarus* had flaked off before the photographs were taken (except in one face, that of Lazarus, where the fine quality of the modelling in the surface paint is still discernible, Ill. 63). What the photograph shows in faint lines here and there, is the preliminary sketch below; and the artists' technique—that of the light, deft sketch, a memorandum simply of the intended lay-out, rather than a precise study to be followed in detail—is analogous to that of a drawing in the Bible already examined (Ill.138), made by the later generation of artists. How individual this technique was we do not know. But the comparison seems relevant. The earlier painters worked differently, following the lines of a more detailed drawing with exact precision.

Most of the comparisons, made so far, have been with the Gothic Majesty Master, not actually with the Master of the Morgan Leaf himself. If we do not find comparisons as exact as these with the work of the latter, it may be precisely because he was a great artist, whose work continually developed; the associate was simply a good artist. It is from the Morgan Master, surely, that the solidity of the Sigena paintings derives. It would be surprising if, in a scheme of this kind, there had not been a number of hands engaged. But the work all shows this

166. Head of the Almighty. Detail of Winchester Bible Initial, fol. 131r   167. Head of Christ. Detail of 71, Christ in Limbo, Sigena

168. David. Psalter, late 12th century.
London, British Museum, Royal Ms. 2 A XXII, fol. 14v

three-dimensional quality, so unlike that of the artists' English predecessors: the bodies represented in the round; standing firmly; not simply a stage army of identities; individuals; happier in repose than in movement. These are qualities which the work of the painter of the Morgan Leaf, and of the initials in the same hand in the Winchester Bible, lead us to associate specially with him. And at Sigena they permeate the whole atmosphere.

In detail also the marks of his presence, not only of his influence, are almost unmistakable. The expression of the Angels descending in the Sigena *Nativity* (Ill.160), so different from the Angel of the *Annunciation to the Shepherds* (Ill.61) and surely in a different hand, is to be compared with the angel in another unfinished initial to the Psalms (Ill.159), this time in the Morgan Master's own hand. The shape of the face, the lock of hair on the forehead, as well as the expression, suggest powerfully the work of the same hand at Sigena on the *Nativity* angels. And here I venture to draw attention again to what I regard as the most distinctive feature of his work: that profound solemnity, which so often broods over it: in the Daniel initial (Ill.172); on the Morgan Leaf; in the sleeping prophet Ezekiel (Ill.171). Here and in others also, there reappears the curious contrast with the self-satisfaction which the faces of the younger characters show. The tragic countenance can also be seen in the seated figure of *David* (Ill.168) from a Psalter made for Westminster Abbey,[24] an illumination which bears all the signs of the Morgan Master's hand. Is it possible that he first learnt this tragic manner from a particular small group of mosaics at Palermo, in the Cappella Palatina—or perhaps more probably, actually from the artist who designed them? Here illustrated is St Cataldus (Ill.169) who is lent something of a western air by wearing his mitre.[25] But what is of particular concern here is the sombre expression he also wears. The mosaic, and those of its immediate companions that seem to be designed by the same man, are perhaps as likely a place as any for our Master to have learnt this way of looking at things. Noteworthy also in this figure are the loosely falling draperies and the easy

169 and 170. St Cataldus and SS Gregory, Basil and St. John Chrysostom. Mosaics, second half of 12th century. Palermo, Cappella Palatina

stance. In neither respect had the artist of the *St Cataldus* much to learn from those astonishing figures in the same church, evidently by a great Master from Constantinople itself, who not only designed but also worked the *St Gregory*, *St Basil*, and *St John Chrysostom* (Ill.170) in a technique which, in that medium, was perhaps hardly ever surpassed. In these three figures the artist succeeds in conveying the texture as well as the fall of the materials—materials of a richness and heaviness that is shown with an amazing sensitivity. The tiny *tesserae* in which the faces are modelled allows the drawing to be exceptionally detailed—though there is of course a degree of stylisation well seen in the highlights of the forehead. The stance is easy and at the same time sure. The mood is serious—but it is not, here, 'tragic'. By comparison with them, *St Cataldus* is, it is true, almost an earthy figure; but his designer is a 'tragic' artist. Perhaps the Master of the Morgan Leaf as a young man, sat at his feet, and learnt from him this tragic 'view of life' which the great Byzantine master of the mosaics does not share. At Sigena, as at Winchester, are to be found examples of this same agonising over the world: in the Almighty for example, as he is shown creating Adam—who is made to share his tragic apprehension; or in that scene in which he forbids Adam and Eve to eat of the fruit of the tree of knowledge (Ill.12). In contrast, the faces of Moses and Aaron for example (Ill.41) seem superficial. A close parallel for one of these two can be seen in the Bible (lower head in fol. 131r); there too, he seems too slick to be the work of our Morgan Master himself.

A problem arising here, however, is that of the division of labour in such a scheme of paintings. It was suggested above that the general design (with the inner frames of colour on the arches, and no doubt also the canopies in the Nativity series, and the frieze of curved key pattern which ran round three of the four walls) must be that of a single master mind—whether the subjects had

99

been set by the patron, or not. In the Winchester Bible, the patron's instructions, where they survive, consist of a short sentence in the margin, not naming the figures, but specifying their actions. Here at Sigena, it seems more likely that the scenes and characters were discussed and agreed between patron and designer. But if the Master artist then sketched out the scenes one by one, what was thereafter the division of labour?

The photographs provide some clues. If we follow round the lower ornamental border of the arch on which the *Sleeping Noah* is represented on the left, and, on the right *Abraham's Sacrifice of Isaac* (Ills.36, 37), it can be seen that the fine lace pattern slightly changes its character, where it passes from below the groups of figures into an area of decoration only. The change is noticeable on both halves of the arch in the innermost element of the central large frond of the pattern. Away from the areas of figure paintings, these inner elements are less elaborate; as if the artist responsible for the figures, though carrying out the decorative band below them, had handed over to another man at the point where the figure design ended; a second artist being presumably responsible for the splendid Romanesque monsters towards the top of the arch on either side. There was a like division of labour in the arch displaying the *Expulsion from Paradise* and *Adam being taught to dig*. In the superb pair of paintings the *Forbidding of the Fruit of the Tree* and the *Temptation of Eve* (Ills.12, 13), no such change is discernible, no doubt because here the whole painted surface to the top of the arch, both to the right and to the left, is part of the main theme: Paradise. A luxurious and beautifully formalised Paradise it is. (Only, incidentally, in the scene of the *Expulsion from Paradise* is there to be seen a readily identifiable fig-leaf, so identifiable, even if the story were not familiar. The contrast with the *Judgment of Adam and Eve* at Monreale is interesting. The leaves there, whatever

171. Ezekiel sleeping. Detail of Winchester Bible Initial, fol. 172r

else they may be, are not fig-leaves; which is another reminder that the Sigena painters are constantly observing freshly for themselves.) What the comparison between these arches suggests is that methods of division were not standard. What was done in one painting might be done in the same way, or might be done differently, in the next.

One further complication suggests itself. The particular treatment of the dark clothes in the *Cain and Abel* scenes (Ill.25), closely resembles that in the *Micah* initial in the Winchester Bible:[26] in the floppy looping up of the tunic round the waist, by some sort of belt which the fall of material partly hides; but above all in the white high-lights, like a tangle of wire as they are to be seen in several of the Bible paintings ascribed to the *Master of the Genesis Initial*; wires which often form angular features like narrow peaked triangles such as we often see in the mosaics of this time. The high-lights on Isaac's tunic seem also to have been in this style. Abraham's, curiously, is treated quite differently. Must we allow for the possibility that assistants came in here and there, to work on the clothes—much as they did in the studios of the seventeenth- and eighteenth-century portrait painters? Here at least there seems to be another extremely close Winchester parallel, however we account for its occurrence. It seems that we may have to consider these paintings in terms of elaborate team work, in which three or four different hands were closely associated—so closely indeed that a single scene might be the work not of one, but of two or three of them.

The portrait genealogies are a special problem. Sometimes individual heads give the impression of being drawn from the same cartoon as one used some-where among the other paintings: so *Amon* (Ill.174), in the Matthaean series, seems almost a duplicate of the Moses, in the *Golden Calf* painting (Ill.45);

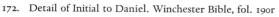

172. Detail of Initial to Daniel. Winchester Bible, fol. 190r

173. Head of Esrom. Detail from Portrait Series, Sigena

174. Head of Amon. Detail from Portrait Series, Sigena

Sadoch, in the Matthaean series (Ill.91) is reminiscent of Aaron watching the Pillar of Fire (Ill.39). *Isaac* (Ill.114) seems again almost a duplicate of the Almighty in the *Giving of the Law* painting (Ill.46) to which, in the original, he is closely adjacent. There is a striking profile used more than once among the portraits (*Iamne* in the Lucan series, Ill.175, and in the same series *Jesse*, Ill.177) which is used also on the *verso* of the Morgan Leaf (Ill.176) for one of David's associates, and perhaps also later, in a wall painting at Winchester.[27] *Esrom* (Matthaean series, Ill.173) and *Salomon* (same series) are evidently done from one cartoon; this offers the chance of assessing the individual contribution. Unfortunately the Salomon has been maltreated by a restorer. In its original form it may have been the more impressive work of the two—more powerful, and as we can see in the face of the child, much more sensitive. One or two of the heads are strongly echoed in a later copy of the Canterbury Psalter in Paris, on the fine *Jesse Tree* page, and sometimes it looks as if the highly mannered Master in that book had been at Sigena. Professor Pächt considers that he was trained at Winchester (by which I take him to mean with the Master of the Morgan Leaf; not perhaps the same thing).[28] All, or some, of these examples may be evidence of the use of a set of cartoons to which members of the *atelier* had access, or of which they made copies for their own use. The work in these portraits is often, even when highly finished, wooden and conventional, and it is difficult to be sure, in spite of the similarity noted above, that any of the portrait artists (if indeed there was more than one) are represented in the main body of paintings. Conventional, the main paintings are certainly not. To compare the scene of the *Sleeping Noah* (Ill.36) with the contemporary version in mosaic in the Cappella Palatina or at Monreale (Ill.178) is surely to be convinced of this. The right arm and hand of Shem, pointing downwards, seems to come from Monreale. But the ruthlessness in Shem's face, compared with the exquisite gesture of his two brothers, each in a different way renouncing his bold invitation to look, is a fine example of the remarkable originality to be found in this series.

To what does this all amount? To the probability, at least, that the Master of the Morgan Leaf, the most distinguished of the second generation of artists who worked on the Winchester Bible, planned the decoration, and himself

175. Iamne. Portrait Series. Sigena   176. Detail of Morgan Leaf verso, 145   177. Jesse. Portrait Series. Sigena

178. Drunkenness of Noah. Mosaic, 1190–6. Monreale, Cathedral

carried out some of it in the Sigena Chapter House, with others of the artists who had worked in Winchester with him, some fifteen or twenty years perhaps after their work on the decoration of the Winchester Bible had been finally abandoned.[29] Their number included the 'Gothic Majesty' Master. The group may have been larger. Similarities with the work of the Genesis Initial Master have been quoted, but only in a narrow field (the treatment of some draperies and the almost exactly similar form of the bursting glory); and I have never been certain that he painted at Sigena, though so much of the iconography seems to be directly derived through him. In his work at Winchester, the faces give him away almost at once. The number of types is very limited, and they are repeated over and over again. I do not see any of them, for certain, at Sigena. It is, however, perhaps worth noting here a point I am discussing elsewhere in more detail.[30] Associated with this later group of artists in the Bible was a rubricator who produced for it a number of magnificent inscriptions in a style which, till his arrival, had not been practised at Winchester—though it was not in fact by any means new. He may also have been a figure painter, though that cannot now be determined. All that can be said is that he, like the Morgan Master, does not belong to the first generation of artists working on the Bible; but that whoever was in charge of the project, at the time of his arrival, thought his work sufficiently important to arrange for the erasure of the first four lines of inscription with which the book opens (the *titulus* of the Letter from Jerome to Pope Damasius), to be redone in the new hand. This commission seems to imply a lofty assessment of the value of his work—of its kind, indeed, unsurpassed. The lettering under the heads in the portrait genealogies at Sigena, shares some of his most individual characteristics. It is possible that he too worked on both projects, as a member of this remarkable association of artists.

In the *Artists of the Winchester Bible*, the suggestion was made very tentatively that one design was based perhaps on the Cefalù Cathedral *Pantocrator* mosaic, seen earlier by the artist himself, not simply known at second hand. It seemed possible that the use of gold background by this later generation of Bible artists might have been inspired by mosaic practice. Some of the tiny gemlike ornament used by them (in contrast to the bold decoration used by the Master of the Leaping Figures) seemed likely, also, to be derived from mosaic borders at Cefalù or in Palermo. In Professor Otto Demus's definitive work on these Sicilian mosaics,[31] he stated the view that at least two of the artists 'must have seen' the Sicilian mosaics (he mentioned in particular those of Monreale), and Professor Pächt, in his Sigena article, talked of two possible visits to Sicily on the part of these artists (or at least of the Morgan Leaf Master) one antedating his work on the Bible, the other between that and the Sigena episode. Other scholars have been unconvinced of such direct contacts, while not of course denying the powerful Byzantine influence in the later Winchester work.

Because the mosaics are such a majestic series, still to be seen, in spite of many restorations, in something like their original form, we tend perhaps to assume them too readily as the source of Byzantine inspiration. Paintings in a Vatican Byzantine manuscript, one of which has recently been reproduced by Professor Demus in colour,[32] can be a reminder that manuscripts also may have played their part. And with the Morgan Leaf Master, the study of wall paintings, perhaps in Southern Italy,[33] perhaps still farther afield, seems likely. Somehow he amassed experience which caused him to introduce what Pächt calls 'specifically Byzantine iconographic features entirely unfamiliar in English art': the child's bath in the *Nativity* at Sigena; in the *Crucifixion* 'the rare motif of the two angels, the one leading Ecclesia to Christ, the other turning Synagogue away from the Cross'. Demus noticed also that the Virgin is dressed in correct Byzantine fashion, remarked also how the artist places Joseph in relation to the *Nativity* scene, his body turning away from it but his face looking back to survey it (Ill. 179)—a remarkable piece of Byzantine sophistication. All these details speak as unmistakably of a phase in his training during which he absorbed Byzantine ideas, as do other details mentioned earlier, of his English apprenticeship.

And to examine the Sicilian mosaics in detail is to realise that there is here *prima facie* a three-cornered relationship, Winchester, Sicily, Sigena; its elucidation complicated by the fact that when the Sigena paintings were done, all the Sicilian mosaics are likely to have been available, whereas those of Monreale could hardly have been seen by the Bible artists.[34] The Genesis Initial itself (Ill.180) provides ample evidence of familiarity with Byzantine iconography

180. Genesis Initial. Winchester Bible, fol. 5r

181

185

182

186

183

187

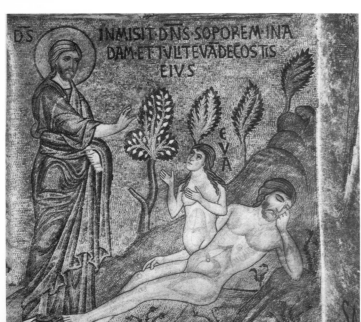

184

Creation of Eve: 181. Sigena
        182. Winchester Bible
        183. Monreale Mosaic
        184. Palermo Mosaic

Return of the Dove: 185. Sigena
        186. Winchester Bible
        187. Monreale Mosaic

188

189

190

191

192 *above*
193 *below*

Sacrifice of Isaac:	188.	Sigena
	189.	Winchester Bible
	190.	Monreale Mosaic
	191.	Palermo Mosaic
Moses receiving the Law:	192	Sigena
	193.	Winchester Bible

194

196

195

Anointing of David: 194. Winchester Bible
195. Morgan Leaf verso
196. Sigena

as well as with Byzantine decorative motifs. It is composed of a series of medallion miniatures set in the tiny jewel-like ornament mentioned already in the context of borrowing from mosaic patterns at Cefalù or Palermo. For our present purpose, however, the significant point is that though at first sight it might seem that the Sigena paintings of the same subjects were (like those in the Genesis Initial) based on Cappella Palatina mosaics, they turn out to be based—where evidence is available—on the Winchester versions of those subjects, not the Sicilian. There exists now only a detail of the Sigena *Creation of Eve* (Ill.181). But it is the detail which occurs in the first Genesis Medallion (Ill.182). The Creator leans forward with a powerful gesture to draw up the woman from Adam's side. In the Palermo and Monreale versions (Ills.183, 184) he dispassionately stands by and speaks the creative word. The moment chosen to represent the Ark, the *Return of the Dove* at Winchester (Ill.186) is one of those chosen at Sigena (Ill.185) and at Monreale (Ill.187). It is true that the rejected raven is not shown at Sigena whereas it was at both Monreale and Winchester, yet the position of Noah in regard to the Ark is the same in the two western versions, different at Monreale. *The Sacrifice of Isaac* appears in the Cappella Palatina (Ill.191), at Monreale (Ill.190), at Winchester (Ill.189), and at Sigena (Ill.188). In all four, the child kneels on the altar, looking away from his father, whose left hand is on his head while in his right he holds a sword. But at Sigena, as at Winchester, the angel catches the sword dramatically to avert the disaster, and points down with the other hand to the ram caught in the thicket below, the ram being accordingly transferred across to the angel's side of the picture. *The Giving of the Law to Moses* comes only at Winchester (Ill.193) and Sigena (Ill.192); but the piled-up mountain beyond him and the radiantly bursting cloud glory in which the Lord appears, are strikingly similar, while there is also, at Sigena, an anointing of David (Ill.196) which has some analogies (e.g. in the shape of the vessel used by the prophet) with that in the Genesis Initial (Ill.194), and with the same scene on the Morgan Leaf (Ill.195). Where the Winchester and Sigena versions differ is in the tension of the older, Winchester, work (particularly when the artist there is the Genesis Master) and the calm serenity of that at Sigena. At Sigena, the Lord quietly offers the tablet of the Law to Moses, who accepts it reverently. In the Winchester version he stretches up eagerly, and the Almighty positively thrusts the tablet at him. Even in the *Sacrifice of Isaac*, the Sigena Abraham is grave and thoughtful, while at Winchester he is a whirl of energy. A detail in Noah's ark of the Winchester version, small though it is, may be nevertheless significant. The slits in the ark there are not straight-sided eyelet embrasures characteristic of the Morgan Master's architectural canopies, but are shaped like the oriental arches of Palermo, and may have been noted there. In any case, the likelihood of the Genesis Master having visited Sicily and brought back iconographic ideas and sketches of Byzantine patterns seems to me not to have been overstated by Demus.

There may be doubts on the other hand, as to whether the classical inspiration which breathes in the work of the Morgan Master, and the Gothic Majesty Master, could have come wholly from the Sicilian mosaics. It is true that the design of the St Cataldus at Palermo (Ill.169), which we have supposed to have influenced the Morgan Leaf Master, shows classical features in the natural fall of the saint's vestments, and in the stance—the right knee slightly bent. And the Byzantine master mosaicist, who worked in the same building, succeeds—in spite of the intractability of the medium—in representing the materials of his saints' vestments with almost incredible delicacy and naturalism. But to see how little this is typical of the Sicilian mosaics as a whole, we should look at some in the Monreale series, the personages seeming to fall forward in their eagerness. Kitzinger talks rightly of the 'dynamic style' in the Sicilian narrative mosaics. There is, indeed, at Monreale in particular, continual movement, and the draperies formalised along certain conventional lines were nevertheless likewise intended to imply movement and flutter. This is the antithesis of our 'classicism'. It is exactly what the Morgan Master sets out to avoid. We see these things still, nevertheless, in the initials at Winchester by the Genesis Master, whose people are always striding, often indeed stumbling, forward as they do at Monreale.

I do not think he had seen—that he could have seen—the Monreale mosaics before his Winchester work. But those fashions were in the air; as were also the different fashions, seized upon by his colleague. If he was in the Sigena team, and indeed painted those draperies with their broken high-lights, which seem to speak clearly of a mosaic technique that he had learnt in Palermo and Cefalù before his Winchester days, by the time of Sigena he had changed most of his ways, almost out of recognition. We may have been misled in supposing him to have been there. But that he too learnt from Sicily, deriving from Sicilian sources the iconographical formulae that he adapted in the Genesis Initial, is surely almost certain.

The probability seems to be that the Morgan Master learnt his painting techniques—for such they are—in the first instance from Byzantine paintings rather than mosaics. The head of the younger man in the group with the grieving David, on the *verso* of the Morgan Leaf, might itself be a fragment of classical painting—though almost certainly the experience must have come to him from his Byzantine teachers. A century later, Cavallini and Toriti were to work in both media, paint and mosaic. The Byzantine master mosaicist, whose work we have seen in the Cappella Palatina, may, similarly, have painted, as well as set mosaics, in Sicily. Or conceivably the Morgan Master travelled still farther east, to assimilate there those specifically Byzantine lessons that Pächt saw in his work. But that he actually saw the mosaics of the Palatina chapel before he worked at Winchester; took from some of the work there his 'tragic' inspiration; sketched such heads as those of the archangels in the cupola of the Martorana Church (Ills. 200–1), heads which later he imitated so skilfully; that he, or one of his associates, copied the *Pantocrator* which looks down the south aisle of the Palatina chapel (as well, perhaps, as that at Cefalù, Ill.203); that he borrowed (for example from the mosaic of the *Raising of Tabitha*, now heavily restored) the Byzantine formula for the expression of grief or anguish, the line of the eyebrows tilted steeply—to use it for Hannah weeping in the initial to 'I Kings' (Ill.198), for Absolom on the Morgan Leaf (Ill.145) and for Mary (Ill.199) in the Sigena *Crucifixion*, that some at least of these things he derived from his experience of those Sicilian treasure houses, I have little doubt.[35]

We are on less sure ground with the debt of the Sigena paintings to Monreale. It seems likely that a detail in the *Sleeping Noah*, already discussed, came from that source. Someone had brought, from that same source perhaps, details that do not appear in the Morgan Master's work at Winchester. There is, for instance, that curious squared jaw, used by the mosaic designer at Monreale (and by other Byzantine artists of about this period[36]) in the *Betrayal* scene; for the face of Judas (Ill.197) and in some other groups also; a squared jaw that appears in many of the Sigena portrait heads (e.g. Ills.102, 104, 111) and sometimes in the main paintings (e.g. in one of Eve's children, Ill.22). There is, again, the odd hair style, in which (as with Joseph, in the Sigena *Nativity* and in many of the portraits) a lock of hair is looped curiously over the ear—a fashion that appears in the earlier Sicilian mosaics also, though not on the Morgan Leaf or in the Winchester Bible. There are thus features which seem to come from Monreale (except possibly the hair style, which could have been copied earlier). But we may not be far wrong to guess that if the Morgan Master himself returned to Sicily before Sigena, the work in Monreale had little appeal for him. It was the spirit of the classical revival that had affected him so deeply; and in the Monreale mosaics that is a rejected fashion.

So our conclusions can be summarised. The great Bible, still in the library of the Cathedral at Winchester, and evidently made for the Priory of St Swithun, contains work representing two distinct artistic phases. The first is Romanesque; the second, a profound contrast with it, in its mood—its 'aesthetics'—as well as in its techniques, was practised by at least three artists whose painting is still to be seen in the Bible; while there is a fourth (the Master of the Genesis Initial) who may also have been associated with the group, and certainly was to a large extent influenced by the new stylistic ideas, though his manner shows strong traces still of the Romanesque tradition.

In the paintings which decorated the Sigena Chapter House, the work of two, or perhaps three of these same artists, seems to be represented. The number would be still further increased, if the later rubricator in the Winchester Bible was not actually one of these three artists (as he may have been), but an independent craftsman; for we see that hand, also, in the series of inscriptions which form part of the Sigena paintings. These artists were powerfully influenced by the mosaics of the Norman Sicilian churches (worked before, or just after, the middle of the century): the Cathedral of Cefalù; and the Cappella Palatina and the church of the Martorana in Palermo; and this influence shows itself already in the Winchester Bible, in the 'artists of the second generation'. Their work in Winchester was done after this influence had affected their styles deeply. In one particular initial, that to the Book of Genesis, in which we happen to be able to compare the same themes as treated in the Sicilian mosaics, the Bible, and at Sigena, it is clear that the Sigena scenes are not copied direct from the mosaic versions in Palermo; but that the designs have passed through the intermediary of Winchester in the process of being adapted for the wall paintings.

We have seen reason to think that the Master whose personality dominated the Sigena work, English though he was, had spent part of his apprenticeship studying in a Byzantine *milieu*. One of his teachers we have tentatively identified

197. Kiss of Judas. Mosaic, 1190–6. Monreale, Cathedral

198. Hannah weeping. Detail of Winchester Bible Initial, fol. 88r

199. Mary Weeping. Detail of 66. Crucifixion, Sigena

200 and 201. Archangels. Mosaic, c. 1148. Palermo, Martorana Church

202. Detail of Initial to Lamentations. Winchester Bible, fol. 169r

203. Pantocrator. Apse Mosaic, 1143–51. Cefalù, Cathedral

with an artist whose work is seen in a few of the mosaics in the Cappella Palatina in Palermo. But he had absorbed not only his aesthetic ideas, but also the painting techniques of this master, or of one of his Byzantine contemporaries. The mosaics had been clearly a new and exciting inspiration. Their superb gold backgrounds in particular, had brought something new into English illumination. Yet it was the possibilities of paint (and, in wall painting at least, the use of gold for the background in this period was not attempted) which were at Sigena exploited so splendidly; so that what the paintings show is not the decorative, and sometimes inhuman, dignity of mosaics, but the humanity of an artist who interprets human qualities not in terms of the dramatic distortion of line, but in terms of living, individual personality.

And our enquiries have brought us into contact with an artist whom we recognise as one of the great masters of his day. After an apprenticeship served both in England and also with some noteworthy Byzantine artist, probably in Sicily, he worked on books for the monasteries of St Albans and Westminster; and when he came to Winchester his arrival there, with an associate who had already collaborated with him elsewhere, introduced a revolutionary change into the style of work on the Bible. Was it perhaps because he worked thereafter for continental patrons that his ideas failed to make as deep an impression as they might otherwise have done, in England? There is one little masterpiece, a life of St Cuthbert, once in Durham, that carries unmistakable marks of his influence. Otherwise both in full scale painting and in miniature, there is curiously little evidence of it. He is to be admired not for the introduction of Byzantine techniques and ideas, but rather because of a new intensity of observation, a new humanity, a new individuality and tenderness in his paintings that make the Sigena *Crucifixion* one of the most powerful, and one of the most lovely works of its time.

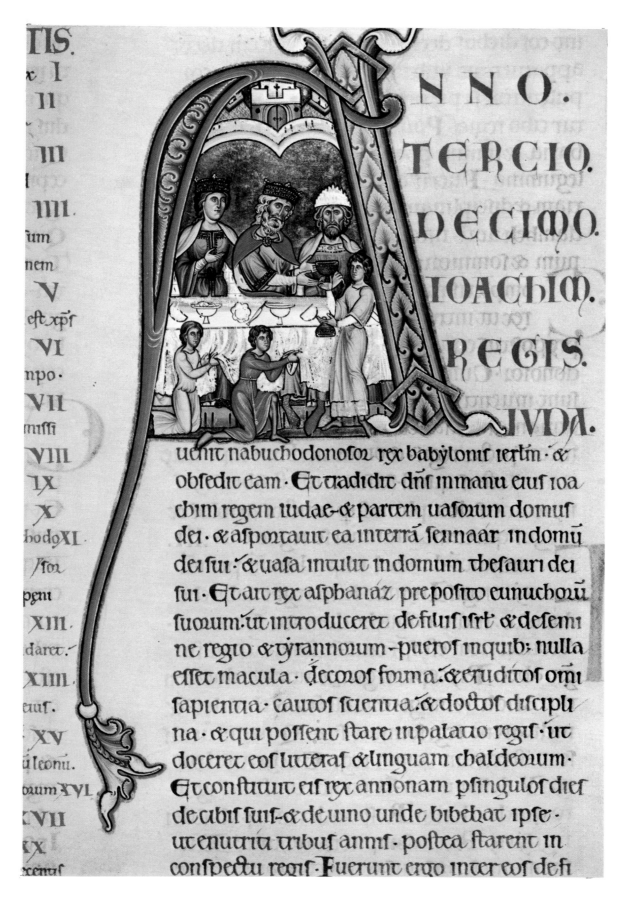

TIS.

x I

II

IIII

ium

nem

V

eft xp̄r

VI

npo

VII

miffi

VIII

XI

X

hodq XI.

/ſor

ogem

XIII.

daret.

XIIII

euf.

XV

ū leoniu.

ōaum XVI.

CVII

XX

cenaſ

ANNO.

TERCIO.

DECIMO.

IOACHIM.

REGIS.

IVDA.

ueniт nabuchodonoſoʒ rex babylonir ierl̄m · &
obſediт eam · Eт тradidiт dn̄ſ inmanu eiuſ ioa
chim regem iudae · & parтem uaſoʒum domuſ
dei · & aſporтauiт ea inтerrá ſennaar indomū
dei ſui · & uaſa inтuliт indomum тheſauri dei
ſui · Eт aiт rex aſphanáʒ prepoſiтo eunuchoʒū
ſuoʒum · uт inтroduceret defiliiſ iſr̄l̄ & deſemi
ne regio & тyrannoʒum · pueroſ inquib; nulla
eſſeт macula · decoroſ foʒma · & eruditoſ om̄ı
ſapienтia · cauтoſ ſcienтia · & docтoſ diſcipli
na · & qui poſſenт ſтare inpalaтio regiſ · uт
doceret eoſ liттeraſ & linguam chaldeoʒum ·
Eт conſтiтuiт eiſ rex annonam pſinguloſ dieſ
de cibiſ ſuiſ · & de uino unde bibebaт ipſe ·
uт enuтriтi тribuſ anniſ · poſтea ſтarenт in
conſpecтu regiſ · Fuerunт ergo inтer eoſ defi

204.   Initial to Daniel. Winchester Bible, fol. 190r

Nativity: 205 (above). Palermo, Cappella Palatina. 206 (below). Sigena

Classicism at Sigena: an analysis of the Nativity Painting

To compare the Sigena painting of the *Nativity* with a Sicilian mosaic version of the same subject, which the Sigena artist must certainly have seen, in the Cappella Palatina in Palermo, is to be aware of the gulf which in fact separates them, and of the originality of the Sigena picture. In the first place the difference is the simple but important matter of the disposition of the scenes in the building. In the Sicilian churches, the scenes of the life of Christ belong to the upper registers of decoration. The Palatina *Nativity* decorates the lower part of the curve of the vaulted ceiling. The *Nativity* at Sigena, as well as the *Crucifixion* there, was brought down to earth. The scenes on the two end walls of the building, as can be seen still in the faint traces that remain in the ruins, were nearest of all the paintings to eye level; and this in itself implies a two-fold difference. At Sigena, the *Nativity* is not simply a decoration, but a narrative; or rather the single moment of a narrative—which is crowded with personalities. In the Palatina, the mosaic is a decoration, the impression of which is designed to convey the remote and un-earthly brilliance of another world, a heavenly world, in which the personages, except in some degree for the Virgin herself and the Child, are dolls, exquisite but depersonalised—as are for instance both the angels and the Magi, whose horses prance into the scene on the upper left while the attention of the riders is focused only on the star. The nurse and maid are tiny figures, who as person-alities hardly tell at all. The Magi reappear in the lower right half, because the picture does not represent one particular moment in time, but rather con-stitutes a descriptive pattern made up of a number of evocative motifs. The Magi were familiar in several contexts: led by the star; visiting Herod; the Adoration; and the dream warning. Here was space in which the Adoration context could be suggested. The figures are reminders, adding nothing whatever to the story they instantly recall. The cradle and the bath are both like rich objects in a ritual. The mattress, or couch, on which the Virgin, a bright figure within the darkness of a cave broken so implausibly into the hill, is somehow managing to sit upright, is clearly again a familiar pattern that helps to translate the whole into the region of evocative traditional ideas. The various elements, the scene of the bath, the arrival of the Magi, the attendant angels, Joseph, are to an extraordinary extent detached from one another. In a sense there is no structure to the whole design except in so far as the various elements are grouped round the larger figure of the Virgin dominating the decoration; the focus of which—the Child in swaddling clothes—is emphasised by the light descending from the star. Joseph is not only turning his back on the scene (for the baby's bath was no doubt a task for the women, not for men) but is looking almost demonstratively out of the scene into the eyes of the spectator, and so separates himself not only from what 'is happening' but from the whole composition, in so far as that word is appropriate here. The effect comes from the scintillating magic of gold and colours. Traditional associations do the rest.

How different is the painting. It is, first, a precise moment in time. True, the cradle and swaddling clothes are there as well as the bath. But there is no baby in them; for he has been taken out of his cradle, and the wraps lie there empty, one corner hanging over the edge of a solidly built, thoroughly mundane cradle, the material of which is clearly wood, though it has the traditional pattern of arches painted on it. The bath is a simple copper, or pewter, vessel, not a liturgical object. The scene is set near the town, Bethlehem or perhaps Jerusalem, the roofs and towers of which appear over the arched frame of the design; which was bounded right and left by pillars, and not allowed to vanish into airy space. As a composition, the painting is boldly centred on the small figure of the Child, and on that of the nurse—somewhat smaller in scale than the Virgin or Joseph, but still large enough (or almost large enough) to be realistic in association with them; certainly large enough for her traditional concern, to discover whether the water is too hot, to be illustrated charmingly and unmistakably, both in the pose of her body and in the beautiful detail of her face. Similarly the concentration of the maid, doing her part also with such care, is clearly represented. We notice at once the careful anatomical articulation of their arms, a most remarkable innovation far in advance of anything in the mosaics—even, in my view, of the Adam and Eve of Monreale. Whether the composition is fully successful, the focus emphasised here by the tripartite arch of the canopy, and by the diagonals pointing downwards towards the centre—

207.   Griffon. Catalan wall painting, c. 1220. Barcelona, Museum of Catalan Art

the edge of the mattress on which the Virgin is here unmistakably lying, her head supported by a pillow; the edge and the structural lines of the cradle; the line that leads through the head of Joseph, and of the maid, and of the nurse leaning forward, to the Child with his halo—is another matter. But it can hardly be questioned that we are dealing with a scene which is deliberately composed, even if it has not yet freed itself entirely from the bonds of a convention which insisted—for instance—that the subordinate figures of the nurse and maid should be reduced in size. In any event, it is surely not fair to judge the painting finally from a photograph that leaves the colours unspecified, and which is all we have. What cannot be doubted is that the Virgin and Joseph are here intended to be human figures, as real and as human as the nurse and the maid, though more important: he sitting with a troubled look turned towards her, yet in deference again to the tradition, his body is set to look the other way; she, in her turn, reflecting with extraordinary grace and tenderness, not perhaps without some realisation of difficulties and dangers, on the future. And above, the angels descending, confident and vital, into the real world; down to earth; saying that all is well. The Child is pointing towards the bath. Is it perhaps, here uniquely in this picture, a symbol of purification, or is this only a human gesture? We notice, in passing, the unusual folds of the long tunic that the nurse has folded back (another real-life gesture) over her knee. These folds seem to be one of a few possible reminiscences of Monreale in the Sigena series.[37] Everywhere there is humanity; and what a singular contrast it was, in the region in which it was painted, to those giant twelfth-century Spanish icons of the Virgin, highly simplified and formidable, in S Clemente de Tahull, and Santa Maria de Tahull.[38] This is, manifestly, a new artistic world; though (as we have already observed) in the triangular-shaped corners of the spandrels, the ornament is still typically Romanesque, and includes a delightful, though limited, Romanesque fauna: a magnificent griffon (Ill.208); a lion, a leopard, a centaur, and so

208.   Griffon. Detail of 37. Sigena

121

on—the limbs of the lion and griffon powerfully articulated in the way the Master of the Leaping Figures at Winchester used to draw them; creatures which set off most effectively the humanity of the figure pieces which fill the more open area of the spandrels. It is noticeable however that ornament of this kind is entirely excluded from the New Testament series. This is clearly no accident.

The great *Crucifixion* painting is, alas, harder to reconstruct. Only details here and there had been freed of whitewash when the photographs were taken. But here, too, here especially perhaps, the humanity of the scene was the fact on which the artist insisted. There is no twisting of the limbs in agony; none of that mannerist, exaggerated, sagging of the body to be seen for instance in the austere but beautiful Romanesque *Deposition* in the Albani Psalter (where the series deliberately omits the actual *Crucifixion*); none of the exaggerated droop characteristic of the Byzantinising crucifixions made in Italy in the thirteenth century, or the mannerist elegance of the Evesham Psalter *Crucifixion* in England. The dignity and the restraint, or reserve, which holds this Sigena artist back from exaggeration, are one of the most important features in what Pächt called his 'classicism'. He goes, in this classicism, 'beyond the Byzantine masters from whom he must have gained knowledge of all those ideas and motifs which they had inherited from antiquity, but had preserved in an adulterated form. Outdoing his masters, he seems to have discovered for himself the inner meaning of the classical message.' And it must of course be true that the medium in which he was working, so much less rich, so much more 'ordinary', and above all so much more flexible than that of the mosaicists, opened up to him opportunities which in mosaic could never have been satisfactorily exploited, and of which he must have become aware through familiarity with Byzantine painting.

Painting Techniques, Sigena and Winchester

Though precision as to where the Morgan Master learnt to paint in the new style, and to use the techniques in painting that went with it, is not possible, much more can now be said about these techniques than was known before the appearance in 1968 of a notable article, by Mr David Winfield, on *Middle and Later Byzantine Wall-painting Methods*.[39] The true 'fresco', that is to say painting executed on fresh moist plaster with which the pigment becomes chemically incorporated when it dries, is Italian; is comparatively late (considerably later than the period now being discussed), and is comparatively rare in its purest form; for surface colour, even in Italy, was often added, after the plaster had dried, *in secco*.[40] True fresco could indeed offer superb, and incomparably lasting, results. But the necessity to provide a freshly plastered area for each day's work made the method laborious. Byzantine craftsmen were evidently aware of the lasting qualities of painting done on fresh plaster, but were normally content simply to moisten the plaster before the day's operations, rather than undertaking the far more elaborate job of separate plastering for each day's work.

The most notable difference however between their paintings and those of western artists, lay in the different methods by which the surface of the painting was built up. In an area which was to be shades of one colour, say a tunic or cloak, the Byzantine artists of the thirteenth and fourteenth centuries began with overall, undifferentiated ground colour. Darker shades of the same colour were then normally used for drawing the folds; sometimes there were two such shades used in addition to the original ground colour. Fold lines were next done in black; high-lights, almost invariably painted in last, in white. Some colours demanded special treatment, the fold lines and outlines on a ground yellow being in umber, the high-lights in a lighter yellow or white. The artist is instructed to mix a particular shade and then use the whole of his mix, wherever, in the series of paintings he was engaged on, it was needed—rather than working up a single area to completion. Drawing of all detail was done with the brush, freehand—not following the lines of an earlier sketch. Sketches in detail had not normally been made, at any rate on the walls, save to some extent for faces—which were anyhow treated differently (as will be seen in a moment) when the time came to paint over the sketches. In the examples in Mr Winfield's illustrations, there are often fairly elaborate sketches for the faces. But for the rest, only the barest outlines were drawn before painting began. Most significant of all, perhaps, is that no attempt was made to tone down the sharp line separating the intermediate shade from the lighter.

Faces and flesh however, are the exception. For those, a much wider range of colours was used, and though the high-lights, or the red of the cheeks, often can be seen as clearly defined areas of colour, the boundary lines sharp, the white high-lights showing as distinct lines, most of the painting on faces shows a careful modulation that makes it impossible to see where the transition between one colour and another occurs. They merge imperceptibly.[41] What the Byzantine artist did for faces in his paintings, the Italian artist of the *trecento* aimed at achieving throughout the work. 'They modelled, the Greeks built.'[42]

In fine quality Byzantine work of the twelfth century hard black outlines are tending to disappear, as they did completely from the paintings of Giotto and his followers in Italy. At Asinou in Cyprus, even the earlier paintings (c. 1105) begin to show this; as with the head of the mourning apostle, standing at the foot of the bier in the *Koimesis* (Ill.133). But the precise dark bounding line re-appears as distinctly as ever in less expert painting done in the same church more than a century later.

The information Tristram gives about the techniques of English twelfth-century wall paintings is summary, but clear as far as it goes.[43] The technique of true fresco was of course not practised in our period; but the plaster was thoroughly wetted before the painting was done, and the first coats of paint with some mixture of lime were thus 'knitted to the walls' by a layer of calcium carbonate covering the pigment. If we apply these observations to the pair of wall paintings in the Holy Sepulchre Chapel in Winchester Cathedral (Ill.216), one at least a generation later than the other, the results are interesting. The second painting was done over the first, a fresh coat of plaster being spread over the first, and keyed into its surface by pitting it with the point of a small pick. This is in itself evidence of the importance attached by the painter to the application of his work direct to plaster. He rejected the possibility of simply painting over the old picture. (Pitting done evidently for this same reason occurs in the surface of some of the Sigena New Testament series, Ill.62. Fortunately they in fact escaped replastering.) At Winchester, the surface pigments put on the older painting, *in secco*, have survived well. The medium, whatever it was, in which they were mixed was sufficiently adhesive for them to have been relatively undamaged by the layer of fresh plaster spread over them which has in practice preserved rather than destroyed. The upper painting (the later), exposed for many centuries, has lost almost all of its *secco* surface colour. What survives are the main outlines painted presumably on wetted plaster. The brown of these outlines, which are marvellously sensitive, has sometimes hardened till the texture is almost that of a varnish. But what survives in this way is in no sense a preliminary sketch that could be compared with the Italian *sinopie* (so many of which it has been possible to recover, because the preliminary sketches they represent were done actually on an independent lower layer of plaster, that can now be separated from the upper); but is rather the final drawing of the design; a part of the finished painting, incorporated into it.

The difference between this and the Sigena technique may be important. But it is important also to admit the limitations of the evidence we are forced to use. All that is available are photographs of areas where the Sigena paint had flaked,

209. Raising of Lazarus. Sigena

210. Raising of Lazarus. Mosaic, second half of 12th century. Palermo, Cappella Palatina

125

to help us see what had happened at an earlier stage of the work. We might be inclined to assume at first sight that the clumsily drawn clawlike foot of Samuel, in the *Anointing of David* (Ill.52), was part of the original sketch. In fact it is surely a restoration, like the drawing of the arrowhead folds above it. So are the lower part of the Angel in the *Expulsion from Paradise* scene (Ill.12), and the lower part of the figure of *Moses receiving the Law* (Ill.44); though in both these instances the restorer's paint, washed away from the lower part of the Samuel painting, has survived. The *Moses* immediately adjoins an area of restoration in the portrait series. But a picture from which almost all the painting had flaked, when the photograph was taken, and which was innocent of restoration, was the *Raising of Lazarus* (Ill.209). The iconography once again comes ultimately from the Cappella Palatina mosaics (Ill.210) rather than from Monreale. Lazarus stands up in his grave clothes, under the arch of his tomb. He is beardless, exceptionally youthful. At Monreale, it seems as if the coffin has been stood on end, with the body inside it. Here, as in the Cappella Palatina, Lazarus stands under what is clearly the arched door of the tomb; standing upright while his coffin is on the floor. At Monreale, an attendant, to the left, holds up the coffin lid. There is no such feature at Sigena, where again the Palermo pattern was surely followed. Immediately to the left is a group of mourners, aware as so often in representations of this scene, of the stench of death, hands held to their faces. On the left were Christ, Peter, and other disciples; in Christ's right hand a scroll on which were doubtless inscribed the words in John, xi, 43: *Lazarus, come forth.* Little remains of the figures on the left and, on this side of this impressive painting, few details alas are to be deciphered. On the right, the painting of Lazarus's head and hand was comparatively well preserved when the photograph was taken. From the group of mourners next the tomb, most of the surface paint had gone. But particularly with the figure in the foreground, the rough design with which the painting began can be discerned; sketched out faintly, probably (to judge simply from its survival) on fresh, or moistened, plaster. It seems to have gone into little detail, though the way the sleeve was to be treated shows clearly. And what may be significant too, though this is not certain, is the line of the neck in the tunic, the shadow of the tunic being noticeably different from that of the uncovered neck. This could have been due to the application of the first coat of colour for the tunic while the plaster was moist; the colour being thus to some slight extent absorbed by it. The faces and hands by contrast were evidently simply surface colour.

There is at Winchester another initial (Ill.212) in a state similar to that of the unfinished pair in the Book of Psalms (Ills. 159 and 211); the original designs, as there, earlier, but the unfinished painting this time by the Gothic Majesty Master. The technique in both is similar, in that both artists begin by painting out the original drawing almost completely (though they are going to follow its general lines) with undercoat paint according to the final colours they propose to use. One of the faces has in part been worked up. There are no bounding lines to it. They would have been put in at the final stage (as must have happened with the Lazarus painting; certainly, in the Sigena paintings as a whole, as with Byzantine paintings, these bounding lines represent the final stage, to sharpen up the image, not the initial framework within which the artist paints from the start). A difference in the practice of the Morgan Master and that of the Gothic Majesty Master seems to be the use by the latter of green to underlie the shadows in the face. There seem no traces of this in the Morgan Master's half-finished initial. It could have come later in the process; but on the whole the explanation that there was a difference of technique seems likely, since one of the Psalms initials is more nearly finished than the Gothic Majesty Master's initial. And the Psalms initials show precisely the Byzantine technique of building up colour. Thus in the oddly shaped blue garment[44] worn by one of the personages in the more nearly finished initial, there is to be seen the darker shade, clearly defined and not modulated into the paler, painted over the first coat of paint. In the right-hand initial, much less far advanced towards completion, we see the undifferentiated surfaces of the first pale coats of paint. The left-hand initial already has some of the white high-lights. The black fold lines are still to come.

The conclusion here, in spite of the fact that photographs only are available of the Sigena work, seems fairly clear: that the methods followed by the later Bible Masters as by those of Sigena are largely Byzantine, and likely to have been learnt actually in the workshop of a Byzantine artist. And, if we say 'largely' the reservation is intended to apply to the use of gold (which in the wall paintings is at this period not yet relevant). In that particular matter the Morgan Master seems to have developed wonderfully successful methods of his own; which consisted basically in building up first a solid background, on the vellum, of a sort of gesso in the areas to be covered with gold. As with the iconography, then, while the Eastern tradition is powerful, there are some ways technically also in which he shows himself entirely independent of it.

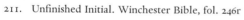

211. Unfinished Initial. Winchester Bible, fol. 246r

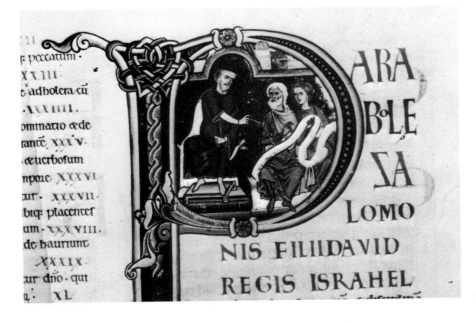

212. Unfinished Initial. Winchester Bible, fol. 260r

213. Detail of 212

214. Detail of 212

215. Detail of 211

216. Deposition and Entombment. Wall paintings, 1170–80. Winchester Cathedral, Chapel of the Holy Sepulchre

The newly uncovered Wall Painting at Winchester, and the Problem of a Winchester School

One of the problems to which the matters here discussed give rise is that of the validity of talking in terms of a 'Winchester School'. There is, elsewhere, a case for a Durham School (for instance) at this period. The fine Pudsey Bible there, which seems to be contemporary with the 'second generation' work at Winchester,[45] is remarkably uniform, both in its illuminations and in its rubrication; and there are other books still belonging to the Cathedral Library, to which they have descended from the library of the monastery, which share the same characteristics. In the Winchester Bible alone, on the other hand, the styles are very various; and one of the earlier styles (as has been noted already) is associated with St Albans, not only because the hand responsible can be recognised in a book that belonged to St Albans, but, more impressively, because many of its characteristics can be traced in earlier work executed in that monastery.

A similar connection with earlier work, this time at Winchester, can be seen in the style of the early 'Master of the Leaping Figures' in the Winchester Bible: the supposition that he was trained in the *atelier* of the master hand in the so-called St Swithun's Psalter (Brit. Mus. MS Cotton, Nero C IV), has much to commend it. But the work of the second generation of Bible artists is a different matter. The methods, as well as what might be called the intention, are then utterly different from those of the Master of the Leaping Figures.

We are bound to ask accordingly whether the connection of the Morgan Leaf Master with Winchester was due to anything more than accident. He and his partners are found as we have seen working in a remote corner of Spain, as well as visiting Sicily. Was the association with Winchester (as presumably with Sigena) based purely on the economic advantages which the patronage of a rich institution offered? Had they been attracted to Winchester by the possibilities of a profitable commission? Or were they trained there?

Something like the economic explanation may indeed be right. But two pieces of evidence now available suggest the need for caution before the old idea of this 'Winchester School' is finally rejected. The first, and more important, is the wall painting recently uncovered in the Chapel of the Holy Sepulchre in Winchester Cathedral; the second is manuscript evidence to be considered later.

The wall painting in the Chapel of the Holy Sepulchre belongs to the latter half of the twelfth century, and the questions of its relationship to the Bible on the one hand, and to the Sigena paintings on the other, are still tantalisingly obscure. The story of its 'discovery' (always a most misleading word in this context) is perhaps worth recording. In 1939, being asked to write an article for the Cathedral *Record*, I chose as its subject *The Winchester XIIth-Century Bible and the Paintings in the Holy Sepulchre Chapel*. By that time, the conclusion that the completed paintings in the Bible had often been painted by an artist different from the man responsible for drawing the original design was already formed in my mind. The pressures of changing fashions, it seemed, might be the explanation why that happened (and this indeed may be part of such explanation). It was of some special interest, therefore, to find that the plaster of the famous *Deposition* and *Entombment* paintings in that chapel, had in two places at least broken away sufficiently to show some sort of painting on the wall below. I thought at the time, wrongly, that it was on the actual stone of the wall; it is in fact on a layer of hard plaster applied to the stone. The surface clearly had been chipped to key in the upper layer of plaster that carried the later painting. But there were indications nevertheless that the colour was well preserved. Accordingly I wrote that the colours of the earlier painting were apparently remarkably fresh, and that 'the earlier painting must presumably be that rarity, a wall painting of the mid-twelfth century; and its existence under the plaster that holds the wonderful painting of the *Entombment* is a strange parallel to that of the drawings underlying some of the Bible miniatures. No doubt it also has been well preserved by the plaster above it, as the magnificent St Paul, in Canterbury Cathedral, of approximately the same date, was preserved by a buttress built against it.'

It seemed important to get the views of Professor Tristram, who knew the upper painting well, and who in cleaning it had of course independently noticed the earlier painting underneath the upper layer of plaster. He mentions it in his book, which appeared some years later. In answer to the question whether there was a possibility of lifting off the upper painting undamaged, to reveal the lower, his answer was that techniques were not sufficiently good to be sure of success. It was therefore a particular satisfaction when, a quarter of a century later, the Trustees of the Pilgrim Trust agreed to finance the operation by Mrs Eve Baker that has ended successfully, bringing to light a painting which is not only one of the most interesting, but aesthetically one of the most important of its time. Mrs Baker's work shows us a painting which like the designs in the Bible initials that are composite, represented the same subject, but the same subject treated in a different way, from the later painting. But here it seems certain that the reasons for re-doing the work were major architectural alterations to the chapel, that involved cutting away a large part of the earlier painting. It had to be altered, to fit into a smaller, differently shaped space.

The painting, like the one that replaced it, is in two registers, an upper and a lower. It represented, above, the *Deposition* and, below, the *Entombment* (Ill.216). The upper register (of the *Deposition*) was divided into two, by the vertical of the cross, along the line of which, in each side, was an inner frame of red; within this the background was blue. These inner frames, as has been noticed already, are a

132

feature of the Sigena designs. On the left, here, is the figure of Joseph of Arima-thaea, with the body of Christ in his arms. His right hand supports the body under its right shoulder, while his left reaches across to make the hold secure. The embroidered, jewelled, hem to his tunic is what we find constantly in the later Bible illuminations (not in the earlier) and at Sigena. The right foot of the body has not yet been released from the nail that pins it; a large pair of pincers is being used to take out the nail, by a figure, sometimes called Nicodemus, standing on the other side of the Cross—as in the later painting. His attitude is tense and dramatic, full of movement. Behind this man stands St John, tall, youthful, leaning forward; behind him again stands the Virgin; who is shown in a tunic, of a pale mauve, above the white skirt (the shadows on which are buff), a tunic decorated with a diamond pattern similar to one on the cloak worn by Zacharias in the *Presentation* scene at Sigena. Her pale blue cloak is decorated with red stars, and the skirt falls round the feet in a way that is characteristic of this group of artists. Unfortunately, the upper half of the Virgin's body was completely destroyed when the new vault to the chapel was made. On the cloak can be seen traces of the triangular patterned white high-lights that we see in the Genesis Initial Master's work. The cloak of the figure with the pincers has, as lining, the 'ermine' or vair pattern we see, in the Bible, lining Isaiah's cloak. The dusted white high-lights on this cloak suggest a phase in which the tech-nique was not yet as stereotyped as it became in the Genesis Master's work. The ground billows with the smoke-like convention that recurs again and again at Sigena, and which is seen, in the Bible, in the work of the Morgan Leaf Master,

218. Detail of 216, Entombment

as well as in the Isaiah initial. The structural alterations that were the occasion of the painting of the second version destroyed all the upper part of the painting above the arms of the cross, and the right and left margins also. Accordingly it is not possible to tell whether there was an architectural canopy, or not, to the upper half of the painting.

The *Entombment* painting, on the lower half of the wall, is bordered, along its upper edge, with such a canopy; a broad, flattish, machicolated arch reaches across the centre, as in some of the illuminations in the Paris version of the Canterbury Psalter (the main artist in which is judged by Pächt to have been trained in Winchester—a judgement which can, I believe, be supported by further evidence). Behind the arch are the roofs and turrets of Jerusalem. These are not in a hand which I recognise, either in the Bible, or at Sigena.

The picture itself shows three scenes. Apart from the *Entombment* in the centre, there are, on the left, the *Holy Women*. An angel, whose wing spreads above, and partly in front of the arch, points out the empty tomb. The tomb, with the group of sleeping soldiers is to the left of, and below, the sarcophagus in which the body is being placed. The chain armour of the soldiers is shown by a convention that is used on the Morgan Leaf and in several other Bible initials of the later phase—never in the earlier. It is not the normal convention used elsewhere in English painting of the period, as a glance at Tristram's plates shows.[46] The group on the right represented the appearance of Christ to Mary Magdalene in the Garden. In the later painting, this group was transferred to the adjoining, south wall, no doubt to give the artist more room for it.

In the main scene, the body lies stretched at full length. The loin cloth is white and buff, and it was a corner of this, overlapping the edge of the sarcophagus, which Tristram saw, in a gap in the plaster covering the painting as a whole, and thought to be the lower corner of a mandorla. By Christ's head is Joseph of Arimathaea, a pillow (it seems) in his left hand. The lines of this figure, again, were closely followed in the later painting. The Virgin, in the centre, holds up to her lips the left hand of Christ; her grief is movingly shown, as is the care of the two disciples on the right, one of whom holds an ewer of the type we see elsewhere in these paintings—in the *Anointing of David*, for instance, both on the Morgan Leaf and at Sigena. Above the Virgin is an exquisite censing angel. This painting as a whole is marvellously sensitive, and there may be a deliberate contrast with the rough, more homespun quality of the scene above. They are divided by a geometric pattern, the centre line of which has for some reason (perhaps because the original line was not level and had to be corrected) moved several inches lower than at first planned. The circles in this pattern are incised with the point of the compass. This is the only use of incision I have noticed in the painting. Though the quality is so fine, and though detail after detail (like the censing angel, to be compared with that in the Psalms initial, Ill.159, and a similar angel at Sigena) is strongly reminiscent of work by others in this group of artists, the hand is not one to which I feel at all secure in attributing any other work, either at Sigena or in the Bible. It must nevertheless belong almost exactly to the period of the later generation of Bible artists. The drapery is naturalistic. The humanity and tenderness of the lower picture is amazing, for its period. Only in the men's faces in the upper register are we aware of strong reminiscences of some of the Romanesque types in the Bible illuminations; for the most part, the work groups itself unmistakably with the later generation.

The new painting at Winchester, then, is in a style sharing many features with the Sigena work, as well as with the illuminations of the Morgan Leaf Master in the Bible (though like that, no doubt distinctly earlier than the Sigena paintings). There are no wall paintings among the many scores illustrated by Tristram, from the twelfth or thirteenth centuries, that seem at all close to these in style. And here another piece of evidence demands consideration: the manuscript copy of Zacharias Chrysopolitanus in the Cathedral Library. The connection

135

of this with the 'second generation' of the work on the Bible is established securely by the fact that some of the decoration is, as it seems to me, in a hand responsible for some at least of the later decoration in the Bible.[47] The subject of the one historiated initial is the winged creature with the four heads (man, lion, bull and eagle) which symbolises the Four Evangelists (Ill.219), and the version of it is strikingly similar to that in the Ezekiel initial in the Bible by the Master of the Morgan Leaf or one of his closest associates (Ill.220). We notice, as characteristic of the Morgan Master, the freely falling folds of the tunic; the face with its curious youthful insouciance, so like the Morgan Leaf Master's painting, though the workmanship here is rougher; the way the wings are drawn, this again entirely different from their treatment by the earlier Bible masters, but taken it seems from Siculo-Byzantine examples as in the Morgan Master's work. It is difficult to be certain here that this coarser piece is not, nevertheless, by the Master himself. It is at any rate in his general manner. So that now, in addition to his initials in the Bible, there are the new wall painting and this Zacharias initial, in another Winchester manuscript, each in a style close to his. The fact that the wall painting is almost certainly not by him, and the Zacharias initial possibly not (though both are close to his work) suggests that the style has more intimate links with Winchester than those of a purely economic connection: as if a great artist and several of his associates were working there over perhaps a considerable period. Among these associates I would certainly count the so-called Master of the Gothic Majesty, who undoubtedly worked, nevertheless, on books for monasteries other than Winchester, as well as on the Winchester Bible.

219. Initial. Winchester Cathedral Library, Ms. VIII, fol. 11r

220. Initial to Ezekiel. Winchester Bible, fol. 172r

Evidence of the Inscriptions for the Relationship of Sigena to Winchester

There is further evidence of a different kind to link the Sigena paintings with the Master of the Morgan Leaf and his associates. A study of the rubrication of the Winchester Bible makes it clear that, with these artists, a new and outstandingly beautiful style of lettering was introduced for the rubrication: for setting out, that is, the coloured letters which accompany the single illustrated initial at the beginning of a book or preface (letters which complete the word to which the initial belongs, and often add two or three more words in colour of the opening phrase); for providing the *explicits* and *incipits* at the end of a book or preface, and the beginning of the next; and for working the coloured initials in the margin to mark new paragraphs, or the running titles in colour, at the top of the page. All these are together a great decorative feature of the book. In the Winchester Bible, this rubrication was evidently planned, originally, to be done throughout by a scribe who worked in the tradition of square capitals. Like other rubricators of his time, he regarded the use of different forms of the same letter, A, C, or E for example, in the same inscription as adding to its beauty and interest. Accordingly he does not invariably use the squared form of these letters, but will write Є, for instance, in the same inscription as E. Nevertheless, by contrast with the new style appearing with the Morgan Leaf Master, 'square capitals' is a fair general description of his style.

When the first phase of work on the Bible came to a standstill (we cannot now ascertain why), Volume I was evidently in a similar condition to what we can still see in Volume II, since unlike the first volume that was never completed: many illustrations begun but not yet finished; many places where the space for the actual illumination was blank, but the rubrication of the remaining letters of the first word had been done; and some where neither rubrication nor illumination had yet been started. Part of the assignment given to the Morgan Leaf Master and his team was, evidently, to complete Volume I. Thus we find a new rubricator, working in a style that seems to be based on the uncial alphabets, and has few points of similarity with that of his predecessor, supplying occasional running titles at the tops of pages from which they had been accidentally omitted earlier; we find him supplying occasional paragraph capitals in colour, in the margins—again no doubt where there had been accidental omissions before. We can detect him sometimes supplying a missing number in a series, since the different form of the letter X he uses, with a broken back,

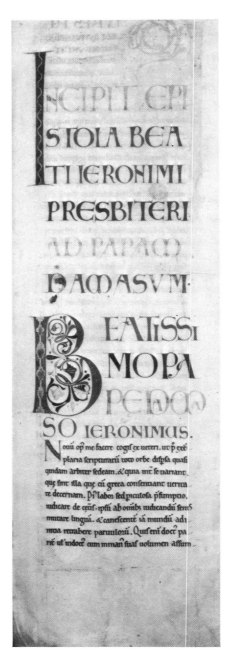

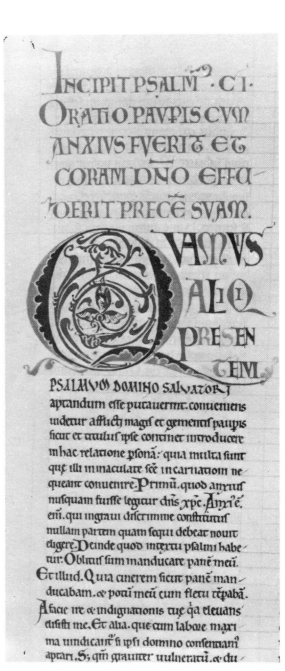

221. Square Capitals type lettering, c. 1145.
Bury St Edmunds Bible.
Cambridge, Corpus Christi College, Ms. 2

222. Beginnings of uncial type lettering,
c. 1165–70. Dover Bible.
Cambridge, Corpus Christi College, Ms. 4

223. The Rubricator of the
Winchester Cassiodorus, 1170–80.
Winchester Cathedral Library, Ms. IIII

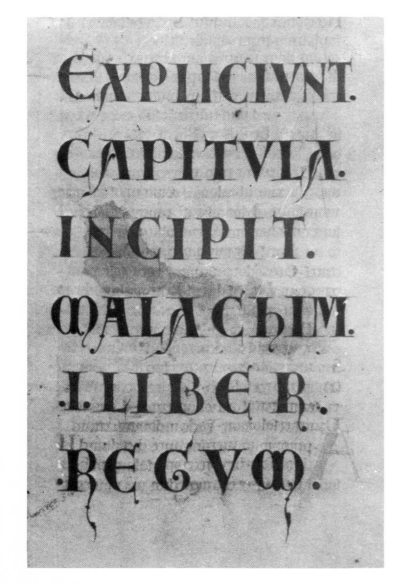

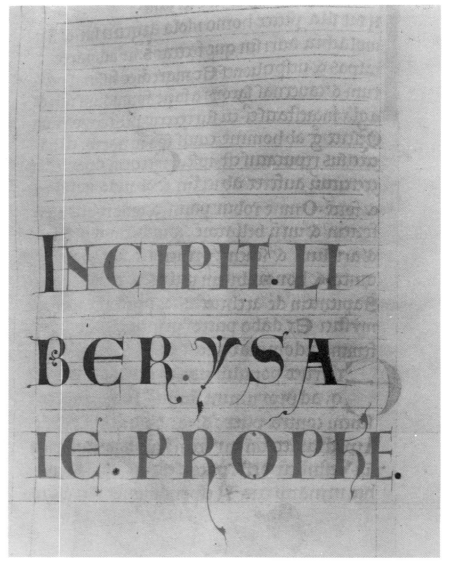

224. Titulus for III Kings. Winchester Bible

225. Incipit to Isaiah. Winchester Bible

is readily distinguishable from the straight lines of the square capitals rubricator. Where all the work still remained to be done (as at the opening of III Kings) he not only rubricates the initial, but supplies a superb 'titulus': the whole providing a magnificent example of the new style. We find him also, for the Book of Ruth certainly (and probably elsewhere also), erasing the rubrication of the square capitals rubricator, because of some mistake in it, and then rubricating the illumination afresh in his own hand. And, most extraordinary of all, we find him erasing the square capitals of the first fine *incipit* inscription with which the volume opens, and supplying them in his new, and so different, hand. (In this particular instance, the remainder of the rubrication—that is to say, the lettering completing the words which the opening illumination, the F of *Frater Ambrosius* etc., begins—has been left in the old square capitals; presumably because the initial had already been illuminated when the later rubricator came on the scene, and it would have been difficult to erase this part of the rubrication without spoiling the illumination beside it.) This most unusual procedure, the repainting of the first four lines in the new style at the very opening of the book, must surely show that the patron responsible for planning the resumption of the work, attached considerable importance to the quality of this new style of lettering.

And rightly so. In some ways the new style is simpler. Only two colours, blue and red, are used, and the not very satisfactory green[48] of the square capitals rubricator is completely abandoned. Again the letter forms vary. In a simple *titulus* of four lines, there may be three or four different forms of A. This again is a calculated effect, as much as is the uniformity of a modern inscriptional alphabet. The letter forms, as mentioned already, probably derived originally from old uncial alphabets, and are accordingly curved rather than square. The quality is far more consistent than that of the square capitals rubricator, whose work can be, by comparison, almost shoddy. In the rare places where a complete *titulus* of four or five lines in this hand is seen, it is superlatively fine: painted, surely, rather than written, and the flourishes, often added to 'top and tail' a letter, of exceptional delicacy.

What concerns us here however is not simply to establish the independent identity of this style in the Bible rubrication, but to note the similarity between it and the lettering below each of the Sigena portraits. And similarities in themselves are clearly not enough, when they occur also in lettering elsewhere in

226 and 227. Inscriptions. Portrait Series. Sigena

the period. They are the marks of fashion, not of individuality. Accordingly, several other contemporary, or nearly contemporary, styles of rubrication are here reproduced for comparison. One feature of the uncial rubricator's lettering in which he seems consistent, and which characterises the curved form of the letter M whenever he uses that form, is a central spool round which the curves are built, having at the top and bottom a rounded 'nose' as it were. This seems to occur, in the curved uncial form of the letter M whenever it is used by this man, at Winchester; and it seems to occur with the curved form of the letter M at Sigena also, without exception. It is very unusual, perhaps non-existent, in similar alphabets of the period, though we occasionally find the 'nose' at the top, but not at the foot, of the spool. The spool with the rounded nose at the foot (but here only at the foot) occurs also as the upright in the somewhat similar letter U, both at Winchester and at Sigena. This is a tiny point; but seems to be the mark of a single individual. If occasionally (as with the letter Y for instance) a form used at Sigena seems to elude us at Winchester, we generally have only to look again to find it, or something so close that the difference is not significant. An exception, however, that appears sometimes (not by any means invariably) at Sigena and never, I think, at Winchester, is the splitting of the horizontal element half way up the letter B, into two curves, before it reaches the vertical of the stem. The Winchester rubricator does use this trick with the similar letter R. But we do not find him using it with B. Yet, since there is no doubt of a substantial time gap between the Bible and Sigena, and since other forms of this letter used in Winchester are so closely paralleled at Sigena, it does not seem far-fetched to explain this as some modification happening in course of time in an individual style.

To explain other mannerisms which do occur both in the work of the uncial rubricator at Winchester and in the Sigena inscriptions, without assuming identity of hand, is not easy. I have in mind in particular the invariable use of punctuation in some form, whether above the line or on the line, between each separate word in an inscription—a usage that occurs both with the uncial rubricator at Winchester and with the Sigena inscription writer. This is not indeed entirely unknown elsewhere, but is unusual. Neither of the other two identifiable rubricators who work in Winchester in the second half of the twelfth century show it. We may draw attention also to the mark by which it is noted that a word is being abbreviated; or to those elegant 'tops and tails' to some of the letters, already observed, something which is so clearly the work of a painter using a brush, rather than a scribe using a pen. On points such as these, we are surely concerned with the idiosyncrasies of an individual. If we conclude that the man who did the Sigena lettering and the later Winchester rubricator were the same, and that he was painter rather than scribe, I believe there is an almost unanswerable case for both conclusions.

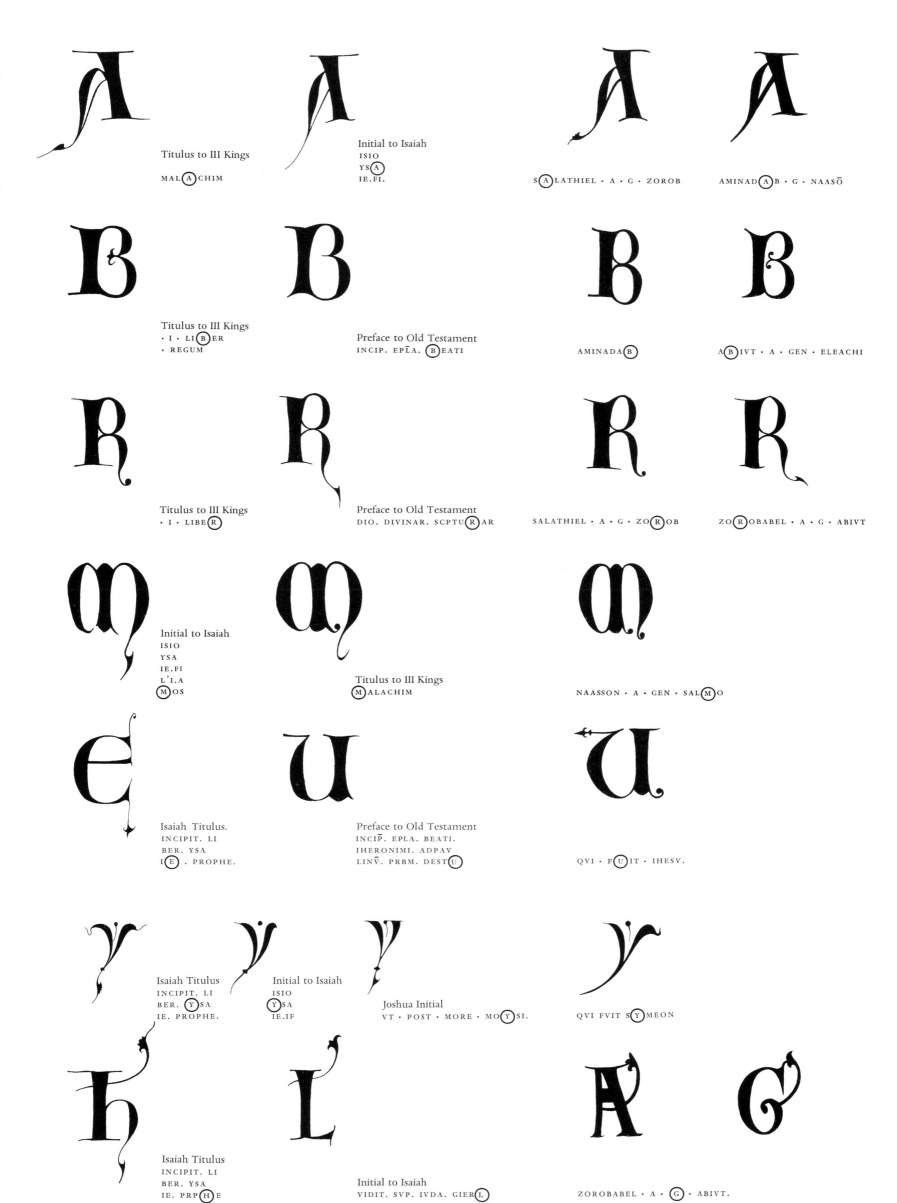

WINCHESTER   SIGENA

Titulus to III Kings

MAL(A)CHIM

Initial to Isaiah
ISIO
YS(A)
IE.FI.

S(A)LATHIEL · A · G · ZOROB   AMINAD(A)B · G · NAASŌ

Titulus to III Kings
· I · LI(B)ER
· REGUM

Preface to Old Testament
INCIP. EPLA. (B)EATI

AMINADA(B)   A(B)IVT · A · GEN · ELEACHI

Titulus to III Kings
· I · LIBE(R)

Preface to Old Testament
DIO. DIVINAR. SCPTU(R)AR

SALATHIEL · A · G · ZO(R)OB   ZO(R)OBABEL · A · G · ABIVT

Initial to Isaiah
ISIO
YSA
IE.FI
L'I.A
(M)OS

Titulus to III Kings
(M)ALACHIM

NAASSON · A · GEN · SAL(M)O

Isaiah Titulus.
INCIPIT. LI
BER. YSA
I(E) . PROPHE.

Preface to Old Testament
INCIP. EPLA. BEATI.
IHERONIMI. ADPAV
LINV. PRBM. DEST(U)

QVI · F(U)IT · IHESV.

Isaiah Titulus
INCIPIT. LI
BER. (Y)SA
IE. PROPHE.

Initial to Isaiah
ISIO
(Y)SA
IE.IF

Joshua Initial
VT · POST · MORE · MO(Y)SI.

QVI FVIT S(Y)MEON

Isaiah Titulus
INCIPIT. LI
BER. YSA
IE. PRP(H)E

Initial to Isaiah
VIDIT. SVP. IVDA. GIER(L)

ZOROBABEL · A · (G) · ABIVT.

Writing line at Sigena 6 cms. wide; at Winchester 1·7 cms. This measurement does not cover 'tops and tails' of the letters.

English Visits to Sicily in the Twelfth Century

The hypothesis of English visits to Sicily at this period may not seem extravagant in view of what is known of the movements of some artists in the twelfth and early thirteenth century: the sculptor who worked in Central France and then at Nazareth; the illuminators from the west whose *ateliers* were established in the Jerusalem Kingdom, and in whose work eastern and western elements are combined; the sculptor whose notebook is in the Bibliothèque Nationale recording his impression of works of art in different regions he visited. Henry II's third daughter, Joanna, married King William of Sicily, the patron responsible for the building of Monreale. It was, by chance, in Winchester that his envoys visited her in 1174, and from Winchester that the young girl set out to meet her husband. Her retinue included nine shiploads; some artists perhaps? The Archbishop of Palermo, who built that Cathedral, was an Englishman, whose long career in Sicily was important, if not particularly creditable. A certain Thomas Brown, leaving a clerkship in Henry I's service, came to Sicily with another Englishman, Robert of Selby, in the first half of the century. Thomas may actually have drafted the foundation deed for the Palatina Chapel in 1140. He eventually returned to England, to become Henry II's Almoner. Robert of Selby also seems to have played a significant part in Sicilian affairs; and, a generation earlier, Adelard of Bath visited Palermo, to produce his Latin version of Euclid's *Elements*. For all these, see the index to J. J. Norwich, *The Kingdom in the Sun 1130–1194*, London, 1970.

Date of Abandoning of Work on the Bible

The text makes the assumption throughout that the Genesis Initial Master could not have seen the Monreale mosaics before he did his work at Winchester. The dates of the Sicilian mosaics are now firmly established thanks to Dr Demus's book.[49] The mosaics at Cefalù, in the Martorana Church in Palermo, and in the Cappella Palatina in the same city, were already to be seen in the 1170's. The Monreale mosaics were not made till the late eighties and early nineties. Precise dates for the Winchester work are almost non-existent. But it happens that the latest completed initial, *Isaiah*, is on a pair of supply leaves, written out to replace the original pair scrapped presumably because of some change of plan. The ink is different, as is the method of ruling, from those of the original. But Dr Neil Ker recognises the hand as being that of one of the correctors who worked on Vol. I of the Bible. He tells me that in his view (which we are not likely to improve on) the hand is of the 1170's. The pages were manifestly written *for this particular illumination* (seemingly as we have said the latest in style of the whole book). I assume therefore that the work was finally abandoned about the year 1180, with 1190 as a 'latest possible' date.

Notes to the Text

1 W. Oakeshott: *The Artists of the Winchester Bible*, 1945, hereafter referred to as *Artists*.

2 O. Pächt: *A Cycle of English Frescoes in Spain*; Burlington Magazine, May 1961, hereafter referred to as *Pächt*.

3 e.g. at Clayton, Suffolk; see Tristram, *English Medieval Wall Painting, the XIIth Century*, 1944, p. 81 and pls. 37–43.

4 See below, Chapter on Painting Techniques, pp. 123–129, where these matters of technique are discussed.

5 The date of this series of paintings has been widely disputed; as with much Byzantine work, the powerful classical inspiration that it shows makes the problem of its chronology particularly difficult. Dates from the seventh to the ninth century have been proposed.

6 E. Kitzinger: *Byzantine and Western Art, XIIth–XIIIth Centuries*; in *Dumbarton Oaks Papers*, 20 (1966) pp. 27–40; and especially his references to Köhler's earlier paper in *D.O.P.* 1, pp. 63 ff.

7 *Development of English Illumination in the XIIth Century*; F. Wormald, Journal of the British Archaeological Association, Third Series, Vol. VIII (1943), p. 44.

8 *Artists*, pp. 10–13, Pls. XXVII–XXXV.

9 It has been pointed out (e.g. *Pächt*, p. 172, n. 42) that this artist's style is associated with the 'classical revival' rather than with the Gothic fashion which was eventually to grow out of that revival. I accept the criticism. But it would perhaps lead to more confusion, if one tried to alter the name now. *Artists*, pp. 15–16, Pls. XXXVI–XXXVIII.

10 *Artists*, pp. 13–15.

11 e.g. *Artists*, Pls. VII, VIII, XI.

12 Probably several more; but the indications of this are not conclusive. In the second volume there were to have been six pages (doubtless finely decorated) of canon tables preceding the Gospels, and a full-page *Incipit titulus* for Acts.

13 Bodleian Ms. Auct. F.2.13; from St. Albans. But the connexion with the Winchester drawings was noted many years ago by L. W. Jones and C. R. Morey: *The miniatures of the manuscripts of Terence prior to the XIIIth Century*.

14 This idiom is seen elsewhere on the *recto* of the leaf, but nowhere on the *verso*. It was used by both the Romanesque masters, the Leaping Figures Master and the Apocrypha Drawings Master; but is never used except here on the *recto* of the leaf when he is following the earlier design, by the Morgan Leaf Master or any of the later generation of painters in the Bible.

15 *Pächt*, p. 175.

16 *Artists*, p. 16. The same point had been made in an earlier article (*The Winchester XIIth-century Bible and the Paintings of the Holy Sepulchre Chapel, Winchester Cathedral Record*, 1939, p. 15) when I spoke of this particular artist 'reaching out to express feelings that are almost beyond the scope of the miniaturist', and of the 'emotional grandeur of some of his figures'.

17 M. R. James: *Catalogue of the MSS at Corpus Christi College*, Cambridge, no. 2.

18 *Pächt*, p. 170; the 'barnacle goose', pp. 169–70; 'octopus acanthus', p. 170.

19 The Pillar is on the extreme right of the scene, along the break in the plaster. In the *Numbers* initial of the Bible (by the Genesis Master) precisely the same convention is used for the manifestation of divine power in the deaths of the three rebels.

20 What seems to be a later, and far more mannered, instance of its use is seen in a painting dated 'about 1230' from Italy, now in New York: cf. Stubbeline: *Byzantine Influence in Italian XIIIth Century Panels*, Pl. III (following p. 101); in *Dumbarton Oaks Papers*, 20 (1966).

21 For an analysis of its use there, cf. Pächt; in the *Hildesheim Psalter*, London, 1960, pp. 106–7. In this feature, somewhat unusually, the Morgan Leaf Master seems to look back to the earlier traditions of the twelfth century.

22 The point can be demonstrated by bibliographical as well as stylistic evidence which I hope to consider in detail in a forthcoming book on the Winchester Bible Artists. For Dr. N. R. Ker's view which I follow, of the date, see below, p. 142, on the date of abandoning of work on the Bible.

23 Cambridge, Trinity College Ms. B. 5. 3.

24 The comparison between this Psalter and the Winchester Bible, in particular the Morgan Leaf, was first made by Millar, *English Illuminated Manuscripts, Xth to XIIIth Centuries*, Paris, 1926, p. 43.

25 Uniquely among the Sicilian mosaics; nor do the near contemporary vested ecclesiastics in Sta. Maria in Trastevere, Rome, wear any sort of headgear. In the Sicilian mosaics Kings wear their crowns. At the end of the following century, popes wear their tiaras in Roman mosaics—but not I think earlier. Otherwise headgear is almost unknown. Professor Pächt and I reached, quite independently, the conclusion that there was a close connexion between the artist of this figure and our Master of the Morgan Leaf. He is inclined to think that the Master actually designed the mosaic figures in question; and he may be right. The western detail here noticed perhaps supports his view.

26 The point can be seen readily in Pl. XLII of *Artists* (the Micah initial); with which compare the tunic of Noah building the Ark, 26 or of Abel, 25.

27 cf. Oakeshott: *The Winchester XIIth-Century Bible and the Paintings of the Holy Sepulchre Chapel*, Figures 1 and 2; in *Winchester Cathedral Record*, 1939.

28 *Pächt*, p. 175.

29 Both the Morgan Master and the Gothic Majesty Master leave initials thus unfinished, as if the contract had ended suddenly, perhaps in disagreement with the patron.

30 See p. 137. Chapter on Evidence of Inscriptions.

31 O. Demus, *Mosaics of Norman Sicily*, 1949, p. 450.

32 O. Demus: *Byzantine Art and the West*, Pl. II (p. 32). Compare for example his Colour Plate II, with the *Numbers* initial by the Genesis Initial Master.

33 As suggested by an example illustrated by Kitzinger, op.cit. (note 6, above), fig. 27.

34 See below, p. 142. Date of Abandoning of work on the Bible for the dating of the Gothic Majesty Master's illumination in the Bible.

35 Demus: *Mosaics of Norman Sicily*, 1949, p. 450, says that 'at least two' of the artists of the Bible, the Master of the Genesis Initial and the Master of the Morgan Leaf, must have been in Sicily and have actually studied the mosaics

of Monreale. I still venture to doubt the Monreale influence, but fully accept the view that the earlier mosaics played a crucial part in their development.

36 By masters from Constantinople itself, working in what is now Yugoslavia, for example.

37 Somewhat similar folds appear in the work there of one artist only: e.g. the lap of the seated figure on the left-hand side of the right-hand panel in Demus's *Mosaics of Norman Sicily*, pl. 73A.

38 These, like the Sigena fragments, are also to be seen in the Barcelona Museum.

39 *Dumbarton Oaks Papers*, 22 (1968), pp. 63–139.

40 'Often': cf. the phrase used by Cennini, one of the great medieval protagonists of the new technique: '*Everything* done in fresco, must be completed and then restored *a secco in tempera*.' Quoted in the excellent technical section by Dr Iago Procacci to the introduction to a notable exhibition catalogue, *Frescoes from Florence*, Arts Council, 1969.

41 cf. Winfield, op.cit., especially colour plate A.

42 Winfield, op.cit., p. 116, quoting from Byron and Talbot Rice, *The Birth of Western Painting*.

43 E. W. Tristram: *English Medieval Wall Painting, the XIIth Century*, 1944, pp. 78–83.

44 Oddly shaped of course because it belonged to the earlier design; which, because gold had been used along the fringes of the tunic, the painter had to follow.

45 It is noteworthy, to take a single example, how often the design of initials is squared. The earlier designs at Winchester are executed within the outline of the letter; or with a letter such as S, its form is the backbone of the design. Some of the later designers liked a rectangular outline; and to set the design against a rectangular frame was an accepted way of bringing an earlier design up to date. At Durham these rectangular frames seem regularly part of the original plan. Bishop Pudsey died in 1195.

46 Compare also the Maccabees Initial in the Durham Pudsey Bible already mentioned, which shows a different armour convention.

47 I have in mind the similarity between the initial C on the second supply leaf in the early text of Isaiah in the Bible; and the initial V for instance at the opening of Bk. III in the Zacharias. The texture of the gold (apart from obvious similarities in design) seems specially significant. Note also the filling in the split of both initial letters; and compare the flourishing in the Zacharias initial with that of the Prologue to Jeremiah in the Bible.

48 Unsatisfactory because it dried in stripes, being put on perhaps with a pen, not a brush, and has a tendency to corrode the parchment. Probably both were reasons for its rejection.

49 O. Demus: *The Mosaics of Norman Sicily*, London, 1949.

List of Illustrations